✿✿✿

PRAISE FOR

ALL FOR LOVE
Annie Benson Müller, Artist & Scholar

More than just a talented illustrator of babies, Annie Benson Müller was a philosopher and teacher, a devoted daughter and wife, and a loving mother to her child and grandchildren. Nyman's intimate portrait of her grandmother is immediately endearing, immersing readers in Müller's day-to-day triumphs and challenges as both head of household in a complex extended family unit and as a female commercial artist in the male-dominated Depression era of early 20th century America. A comprehensive biography that spans Müller's lifetime, *All for Love* is a must-read for artists, romantics, and philosophers alike.

—LYNN BERRY, visual artist, poet, and Art Professor, Notre Dame College, OH

Dorothy Nyman tells a fascinating and inspirational true story about a bright, artistically talented, idealistic woman—the grandmother who raised her—who shows remarkable resiliency, equanimity and optimism no matter what obstacles life throws in her path—and they are many and large. This is a wonderful book!

—CHRISTOPHER FAHY, author of *Chasing the Sun*, *The Christmas Star*, and *Gone from the Game*

All for Love

ANNIE
BENSON
MÜLLER

Artist & Scholar

a biography by
DOROTHY NYMAN

ALL FOR LOVE
Annie Benson Müller, Artist & Scholar

Copyright © 2015 by Dorothy Nyman

ISBN: 978-1-63381-043-3

Original artwork on the cover and interior by Annie Benson Müller

designed and produced by
Maine Authors Publishing, Rockland, Maine
www.maineauthorspublishing.com

Printed in the United States of America

*My eternal gratitude to the One
who nudges me to do more than I think I can.*

CONTENTS

FOREWORD

Four decades after Annie Benson Müller's death, I, her youngest grandchild, am impelled to record her life, for I have never met her peer. Although best known for paintings of babies and children set in idyllic natural scenes, she was also an exceptional scholar. Even at the end of her life, she was striving to complete her thesis on trinitarian aspects of the universe as a unifying principle. She yearned to contribute to the scientific and philosophical thinking of her time and said that if anything she left behind had merit, it was this, and not her paintings. But blindness kept her from completing the work. Sadly, only a number of tapes and incomplete notes remain, but included in the following pages are excerpts from her notes that demonstrate a rare intelligence.

Had she not been an artist or a scholar, the courageous way she met personal challenges alone would ask to be heard. A star-crossed marriage, a broken bond with her only child, the care of three grandchildren, poverty and blindness could not defeat her spirit.

Because she was a keeper of family history and a storyteller, I am privileged to know many details of her life and thought. Therefore much of this story is in her own words. Lastly, I believe that it was mainly her loving presence throughout my early years that enabled me to survive and her example and teachings continue to nourish my spirit today.

chapter one
In the spotlight

It is 1967, and tonight the featured speaker at Boston University is esteemed social philosopher, Jose Ortega y Gasset. The audience files in quietly. Escorted by a younger woman, a stout, elderly woman, carrying a white cane, takes a front row seat. Though nearly blind, her dark eyes are still bright and lively. She wears a smart black hat over snow-white hair. She carries her head high, revealing a striking profile with a well-defined aquiline nose, high forehead and a pleasant expression around her mouth, as though she might laugh easily. Yet, her persona is one of keen intensity, fully engaged in the moment.

This evening is a particular pleasure for her, as scholarly discourse is her favorite activity. She has been a lifelong student of philosophy, physics, astronomy, psychology and parapsychology, natural history, ethics, ancient history, art, politics, anthropology and archeology, to name a few things. Indeed, even topics that do not interest her, such as sports or fashions, still evoke strong opinions from her. Now she settles in and waits for the feast of ideas to begin.

Dr. Peter Bertocci, professor of philosophy at B.U., and appointed to introduce tonight's speaker, steps to center stage. He is a small, congenial man, beloved by his students. "Welcome, ladies and gentlemen," he begins. He scans the audience and smiles.

"Before I present tonight's speaker," he says, "I would like to introduce to you someone I see here in the front row. One of the

most elevated minds I have ever known, and from whom I have learned much. Mrs. Annie Müller, would you please stand up?"

The elderly woman's expression changes from calm composure to flustered shock upon hearing this gracious compliment. She blushes, but manages to rise and nod toward the audience before quickly re-seating herself. "Oh, how embarrassing!" she whispers to her companion, who is smiling and still applauding with the others.

Annie Benson Müller has never been comfortable with public recognition. She especially abhors pride or even the appearance of pride. She once pointed out a drum majorette to me when I was a child.

"Look at her strutting!" she said. "No modesty. You know the old saying, 'Pride goeth before a fall, and a haughty spirit invites defeat.' It's a good thing to remember."

And very soon after, her words became quite clear. At 10, I greatly admired Sonia Henie, the figure skater. While skating on a pond I noticed some people watching me, so I attempted to imitate her famous bow for my audience. But, my blade caught in a crack on the ice and I was smacked, belly down. As I lay there, trying to catch my breath, I fully understood Gram's words.

To live with her was to be taught everything, every day, in every way, just like that. She saw a natural history lesson in a tiny lichen, a science project in a snowflake caught on black velvet, and a moral debate in donating my beloved roller skates to the scrap drive during WWII. She was a born teacher and felt that life was a school. In a discussion about suicide, she told me this:

> We receive our lessons along the way. If we don't learn them, we will get them again and again until we do. Just as in the first grade we must learn our addition before we can manage subtraction, and later we must know addition and subtraction to use multiplication. If

we try to run from our lessons by killing ourselves, they will be compounded as we try to move on. So, doesn't it make more sense to buckle down and learn them as they come along?

And, indeed, she received every difficulty in her own life as a necessary lesson, never complaining or blaming others.

How did she maintain her courage, her joy and her deeply loving nature even in the darkness? I sift through letters and memories to discover what shaped her thinking and choices.

At her birthplace, I find the cellar hole of the old farmhouse, the brook she ran to each morning as a child, the runner of a sleigh that may have carried her from the mountain to her one-room schoolhouse at the bottom. I can hear her dear voice telling me her stories once more. The key events that challenged her ideals, rocked her foundations, shredded her expectations. And the reasons why she believed, in spite of everything, we must 'wake up bright in the morning light, to do what's right with all our might'; that truth was absolute and 'love never faileth.'

Gideon Cushman, Annie's grandfather

Eveline Bicknell, Annie's grandmother

Thomas Benton Benson, Annie's father

Irene, 2, with Annie's mother, Amanda Cushman Benson

chapter two
Mayflower stock

During the final days of Reconstruction after the Civil War, while Rutherford Hayes was President, Annie Belle Benson was born. It was August 1,1879, a hot summer day at a simple farmhouse on Black Mountain in Sumner, Maine. She was the fourth and last child of Thomas Benson and Amanda Cushman.

Thomas Benson's people had come from Massachusetts, where his grandfather had married a Wampanoag woman. Because of hostility at the time toward Native Americans, the marriage was not even recorded in the Benson family Bible. Those that knew the history called his family the 'Black Bensons.' Indeed, Tom had black eyes, which Annie inherited. Local people said that Thomas's widowed mother had come all the way from Massachusetts trailing a wagon full of her fourteen children. As she entered Sumner, she made it known in a loud and jolly way that her boys would be looking for wives.

On the other side of the mountain, in Buckfield, lived an eighth generation settler, Gideon Cushman, with his wife Eveline Bicknell. Gideon's ancestor was Robert Cushman, purser of the *Mayflower* and *Speedwell*. His son, Edward, had lived with Governor Bradford at Plymouth Colony, while Robert was at sea. Gideon's grandfather fought with Washington at Valley Forge, and he and his brother had settled what became Buckfield, Maine.

Gideon and Eveline lived on a prosperous farm with a stable of fine horses in an ample house with white fencing. Eveline was known for her hospitality, often offering travelers tea and pie on her porch. Gideon was highly respected in the area and the Kennebec newspaper would celebrate his virtues on his ninetieth birthday. Amanda, mother of Annie, was the oldest of his six children. How could she have even met Tom of the "Black" Bensons?

Well, Thomas and his brother Calvin were handsome boys, and strong, good workers so Amanda's father had hired them as farm hands. Tom had been nicknamed "Jesusly Tom," by his brothers because of his exceptionally good disposition and Amanda fell in love with him. Her sister Rosabel, fell in love with Calvin, as well. When Gideon realized what was happening he was outraged. Not only were Tom and Calvin not from good old New England stock, but they were "half-breeds" in Gideon's eyes. So he pronounced to Amanda and Rosabel that he would disinherit them if they even thought of marrying Black Bensons. That should end the nonsense, he thought. But, in secret, Amanda simply began stitching her trousseau. She would perch on the windowsill to sew and embroider by the light of the moon. Indeed, both girls defiantly married their loves. And Gideon disinherited both of them. They would be poor, without any land, and forever out of favor with their father. But that did not dampen their love for their husbands and their children, who would be double cousins.

Amanda and Tom leased a small farm in Sumner on the side of Black Mountain. They raised some chickens, pigs, sheep and cows and lived simply off the land, growing vegetables, grapes, pears and apples. Amanda baked beans in a brick oven every Saturday, fried donuts daily and in the pantry, kept a crock full of caraway cookies. At daybreak she cooked a breakfast of pork chops, eggs and potatoes for Tom before he went out to work in their fields and orchard, then she tended the hens, washed and mended clothes, ironed, swept, churned butter, and baked their bread.

Soon their first child was a born. A black-eyed, rosy-cheeked son, Berty, his father's darling. When he was a toddler, the boy and his father played a game each day where Berty would hide behind the door at suppertime, so Tom could pretend to find him. But, one day when Tom scooped him up for a hug, the clasp on his suspender scratched Berty's leg. Soon infection set in, then blood poisoning and meningitis. Darling Berty died just before his second birthday. In his grief Tom blamed himself.

Subsistence farming alone could not support them so they moved to Massachusetts in the winters so Tom could work in the shoe factories there. While in the small town of Abington, south of Boston, their second son was born. Willie was fair with blue eyes like Amanda. But like too many parents of their time they again suffered the loss of their child. Willie was just eighteen months old when he died. This time it was due to an epidemic called 'cholera infantum,' a gastrointestinal infection. Years later, Amanda told Annie that nearly every family in their town lost a child. The church bells had tolled the age of each child that died, and for days it rang 2… 1… 1… 3… 2… and so on.

With their two boys born and lost within five years, their happy home suffered deeply. Tom still carried guilt with his grief. And Amanda was determined never to have another child. So for seven long years she refused him in bed. When she was very old, she told Annie that her refusal had caused Tom to believe she was having an affair. Poor Tom would dash home from the factory unexpectedly and run through the house madly searching closets for her imagined lover. But finally she relented, and their daughter Nell was born. Five years later, while at the farm in Sumner, when Amanda was thirty-nine, Annie arrived. She was dark-eyed and rosy-cheeked like Berty. Perhaps because they were wary of city life after the epidemic that took Willie's life, Tom and Amanda decided to stay on the farm until the girls were older, even though the country also had its perils.

Amanda had taken Nell and Annie, just nine months old, to visit her sister, Rosabel in nearby Paris, Maine. As was the custom, the small cousins had all bundled in the same bed during their visit. A few days later, after they were back home in Sumner, Amanda got a note from her sister. There was an outbreak of smallpox in Paris. Although vaccination had been available since the early 1800s, there was no mandate and many people refused to risk it. But Amanda's fear of losing another child was so great; she had Nell and Annie both vaccinated twice. Amanda said that she regretted not having any pictures of her two little boys, and would not make that mistake again. So she took some of their scarce money to have the girl's photographed, just in case. Her terrible losses had left her a bit fatalistic. She was quoted as greeting any misfortune with a sad sigh of, "Oh, well, never mind." Tom said that if Amanda died before he did, he would be sure to recognize her ghost by that sigh. But, thankfully, both girls survived, and got to spend eight more summers on the farm.

Gram spoke of her early childhood always with such reverence and joy in her voice, that I often wished I had been Tom and Amanda's child too. Here is how she remembered Black Mountain.

> One of my earliest memories was as a small baby about one year old. I was in my crib, ill with a fever and Father was away. When he returned home he had brought me an orange all the way from Boston.
>
> I can still remember its bright color and fragrance, and his strong presence over me. In those days tropical fruits were rarely available to any but well-to-do people, but he would sacrifice greatly for his children. I watched everything he did with adoration, even when he chewed tobacco. It was aromatic with molasses and apple cider.
>
> I thought it must be delicious. So, I climbed up in a chair, took it down from the mantel and bit off a chunk as I had seen him do. But it was awful! I spit it out and

cried because I couldn't believe anything connected with my father could be so nasty.

He would hold me in his arms and say, 'I love you more than tongue can tell.' And I would repeat, 'I love you more than Tunk and Tell.' I didn't know who Tunk and Tell were, but was sure I loved Papa more than anyone in the world.

As I grew, he would take me with him, milking, tilling, planting, and teaching me about plants and moss, insects and birds, infusing me with a life-long passion for the natural world. Walking with my hand in his I felt that even a big thunderstorm couldn't hurt me. While Nell went to the one-room school at the foot of the mountain, I roamed outdoors with our dog, Major, lay for hours on my stomach to watch for life in the pools of our brook. Our cat, Richard, surprised us with many darling kittens. I got to feed Lollypop, my very own orphaned lamb, with a baby bottle. There were pink piglets, the juciest apples, called Yellow Transparents, and fragrant Niagra green grapes.

We would snip a bit of Sweetfern to inhale its scent as we walked. In winter, Papa bundled Nell and I in a red woolen blanket and would take us down the mountain in the sleigh. Evenings, he often read aloud from *The Golden Treasury*, an anthology popular at the time. We heard Longfellow, Sir Walter Scott, stories of the Arabian Nights, or King Arthur. Often we would ask for David and Goliath, Jonah and the Whale, Daniel in the Lion's Den, from the family Bible.

While he read to us, Mother and Nell would do needlework by the fire and I might lie under the table trying to draw a flower I had picked for Mother that day. Once, frustrated because my drawing didn't look like the original, I cried out, 'Why do I HAVE to draw?' Everyone laughed. But for me, at the time, it was a valid question, for I had no idea why I had such a strong urge to draw everything that I thought beautiful or interesting. Always encouraging, Father soon came home with my first box of watercolors and a good brush. He also taught me to memorize and recite long poems. We were rich in so many ways, though we had so little money. Ours was a house full of love.

During my eighth summer, my parents decided it was time I went to school. I already knew how to read, write and cipher from watching Nell. But, I was eager to join her in the one-room schoolhouse at the foot of the mountain. What I was not prepared for were the other children. My only contact with boys thus far had been several visits to my two boy cousins in nearby Paris. They were kind and friendly to me always. But some of the boys at the school were dirty little ruffians. I couldn't imagine why they were so rude and not interested in learning. Those Nell's age liked to tease her. When one of them yanked her lovely long braid and made her cry, I was outraged. As he stood by the water barrel laughing, I filled the dipper full and dumped the icy water right down into his boot. He yelled loudly. 'There!' I said, 'Now you leave my sister alone!' I had quite a temper. I have struggled to control it all my life. But at the time I felt justified, because he had hurt someone I loved.

Gram's lack of social experience throughout her first eight years led to many awkward and painful moments in her school years. Her first few years completed in the little school in Sumner, the family finally moved permanently to Massachusetts. She spoke often of her experience at Abington High School there.

I was two years older than my classmates and a very eager student. In the late 1800's many children, especially girls, did not go beyond the eighth grade. Nell didn't and my father's friends even chided him for urging me to finish high school and go to college, as they said I would never be anything but his daughter. When I heard that I said, 'I'd rather be Tom Benson's daughter than anyone else in the world.'

In our high school we studied Greek, Latin, algebra, calculus, trigonometry, history and classic literature. Most of my classmates were from middle-class families and the boys were either college bound or preparing to take over a family business. I loved my studies and excelled in school, but was often ridiculed by those who did not. When the teacher would ask a question, my hand was always up and someone might say snidely, 'Oh, just ask Annie. She knows everything.' This hurt and embarrassed me.

My first experience of this kind of reaction had happened at home when I was about four years old. Mother was helping Nell to memorize a rhyme for school. I was listening with great interest from the bed in the next room. Nell kept forgetting the last few lines and began to cry in frustration, whereupon I jumped up and down on the bed and recited the whole thing perfectly. This caused Nell to cry even more, of course. So, Mother scolded me for showing off and hurting Nell's feelings. I felt awful, because I loved Nell. But I was also confused, because my ability to easily memorize and recite things had always been praised.

In high school I didn't have a social life per se, except for a wonderful friendship with two boys, Ernest and Allen, who were also serious students. We three decided to learn Morse code and call ourselves the Secret Telegraphic Society. We had great fun sending messages back and forth for a long while. However, toward the end of our senior year Allen sent me a sentimental message, about us being sweethearts. Rather than being flattered, I was totally shocked. I felt that our wonderful platonic friendship was ruined, as I had no interest, or experience for anything else. Not knowing what to say, I simply stopped speaking to him. My rejection hurt him terribly, for he was truly a fine boy and very sincere. Years later, at a class reunion, I was able to apologize.

Except for my cousin Florence, who was also a schoolmate, I did not have any girl friends either. I did admire one very pretty girl, who had a lovely singing voice. I watched her closely trying to understand how she was so popular, because her behavior appalled me. She was always whispering in class and passing notes and showed little interest in the work. Once when we formed a line to file out, she positioned herself among the boys and reached behind to grab them in their crotch, which they seemed to think funny. Sometimes she hastily drew male genitals in chalk as she passed the blackboard. I asked Mother how she could be so lovely and talented and still be so vulgar.

'If a girl thinks about her tippy-whippy all the time,' she answered, 'she doesn't have any brains left to think of other things.' Poor mother. She didn't know what to say, although there is some wisdom in what she said.

Amanda's answer, though amusing in today's world perhaps, really did not address Gram's struggle to find a way to make friends in spite of being exceptionally bright. And equally important, did not enlighten her confusion around issues of sexuality as she grew.

When Nell married at eighteen, Annie was thirteen. It was decided that the new couple would take the bedroom Nell and Annie had shared, while she took a small attic room. On the first night of this arrangement, Annie innocently burst in on Nell and her husband, Otis, to say goodnight. They were naked and very involved in lovemaking. Although she had seen animals copulating on the farm, she was truly shocked now. She ran to her mother for explanation.

"Why are they doing that awful thing?"

"Because we must do evil that good may come," said poor, flustered Amanda. Again, her answer gave Annie a conundrum instead of important information about human sex. What a negative image to hold as she worked her way through puberty!

She often related the following painful episode of social isolation and ridicule.

Once, at the end of a school day, I heard some of the girls laughing together in the coat room. As I entered, I saw my shabby coat hanging up stuffed with towels, like an effigy. The girl I admired was examining it with a look of disgust.

'Whose old rag is this?' she said. 'How awful!'

I was so humiliated that I could feel my face burn. I had never minded that I didn't have new clothes, because I knew my parents gave me all they could. My dear mother had patched one of Nell's old coats carefully to make it last. But now I felt these girls were making fun of my whole family as well as me. I didn't know what to do, so I pretended that I thought it was terribly funny, and laughed along with them, saying, 'Yes, what a funny old coat it is.'

I took down the coat and removed the towels and they all left the room whispering. I walked home the long way alone, went into the town cemetery, lay down and cried my heart out. I never told my family.

At graduation, 1898, Annie was valedictorian and wrote this poem for the occasion:

A sculptor once with skillful hand
Wrought from a piece of clay
A figure fair as summer dawn
From some ideal model drawn
Beautiful as the day.

Then high upon a citadel,
Before a temple grand,
In sparkling marble fair as snow,
It shone across the plains below,
The pride of all the land.

We all are sculptors great as he
As moulding life with eager hands
Far sweeter joy we know as
Christ, our model, by us stands,
We see His likeness grow.

So guided with each faltering stroke
At last our clay shall be
A fairer form than earth may know,
Fadeless and pure in Heaven to glow
Through all eternity.

When I first read this poem, I was struck by its high-minded idealism, but even more by her reference to Christ. Of course her father had read aloud often from the Bible, but she had never attended Sunday school, nor were the family church members. So the threads of Christian doctrine woven informally into her early days must have inspired the images for her poem. The only church experience she mentioned was that she had once decided to join a choir with some of her schoolmates. On the night of the first rehearsal the young people were asked to unpack new hymnals. Some of them decided it would be fun to crack the bindings on the new books, ruining them with great hilarity. Annie had been taught to love books and found this so upsetting she would not return. So again the opportunity for a positive social experience with her peers was lost. I can only assume that she drew her Christ image from her father's Bible stories, and the fact that she taught herself to play hymns upon an old pump organ the family had acquired.

But throughout her life, all systems of belief interested her. She read deeply and remembered what she learned. She had studied Greek in high school and remained passionate about the ancient Greeks all her life, extolling the wisdom of Plato, Socrates or Homer, even to the point of being able to recite whole stanzas of the *Iliad* in Greek when she was in her nineties. The Greek myths and legends with their many gods and plots were stories she knew by heart and often told us over the dinner table to our great amusement. She always carried a small edition of Plato's *Republic* in her purse in case she had to wait for a train or bus. Besides the Bible and Greek mythology, she also read the Koran of Islam, the Hindu Bhagavad-Gita, books of Buddhist thought, works of Emerson and other Existentialists, the Roman Catholic Catechism and Mary Baker Eddy's *Science and Health*. And she stretched her mind around metaphysical theories like Astrology, Palmistry, Phrenology, Spiritualism, as well, seeking answers to the hows and whys of our creation, existence and meaning everywhere.

It's no surprise that, upon graduation from Abington High School, she was offered a full scholarship to Bates College, Maine. Her intention was to continue her studies in the classics—Greek, history, literature, philosophy. However, this was not to be.

Her beloved father had become ill with diabetes and a condition that his physician called, "tobacco heart," believed to be due to his habit of chewing tobacco. The diagnosis of 'tobacco heart' was most probably a circulatory disorder caused by nicotine toxicity combined with diabetes. In any case he suffered from peripheral neuropathy and gangrene in his feet and could no longer work. As Nell already had several children, there was only one person her parents could turn to for support: Annie.

This was the first of many major sacrifices she would make for loved ones. She willingly refused the coveted Bates scholarship and enrolled in a two-year diplomate at Bridgewater State Teacher's College. She had never wanted to be a schoolteacher, but this readied her as quickly as possible to care for her parents. Her father cheered her on, eager to know all she learned, discussing her courses with her and when he was well enough, helping her identify geology specimens. She cherished an amethyst geode that they discovered together during that time. In 1901 she graduated, valedictorian again, and two months later, Tom Benson died.

> Father died at home, as everyone did then. Mother and I cared for him day and night. At the very end he opened his eyes, attempted to sit up and cried out, 'Cal!' He seemed to have seen his beloved brother Calvin, in the room. Of course, Uncle Cal had died several years before. Father didn't regain consciousness again.

Annie was hired as a first grade teacher in Abington. Although she had not wanted to teach, she really enjoyed children. So some of those that were fortunate enough to have Miss Benson in first grade, remembered her with great affection many years later. But, very soon, she recognized that her artistic abilities could greatly increase her earning ability. So she enrolled in the Massachusetts Normal Art School in Boston, and simultaneously got herself hired as the art teacher for several towns nearby, called 'The Abingtons.' That meant taking the train to attend classes in Boston three days a week and hiring a horse and buggy to bring art classes to some four elementary schools south of Boston on the other days. She was now able to pay the rent on a small apartment and provide necessities for herself and Amanda. Even so, Amanda sold lady's magazines and Larkin soap from door to door to help out.

Theirs was a contented life together and not all work. Gram remembered getting tickets for herself and her mother to hear the Adamowsky string quartet, which was playing at Beamis Hall in their town. She remembered this amazing experience.

We saw that Beethoven and Mozart were on the program and knew that they were great composers, but had never heard their music. We didn't even know how to pronounce their names. We knew only the folk songs and hymns of our generation, like "Home Sweet Home" and "Abide With Me." When the quartet played, we were so moved that tears ran down our faces. To this day, Mozart is my favorite composer.

And after that initiation to classical music as a young adult, Gram would find her way to many operas in Boston, sitting in the third balcony. Her record collection in later years contained Caruso, Madame Schumann-Heink, Olive Klein and other great singers of the early 1900s.

While teaching and attending art school simultaneously, Gram had no time for a social life, nor did she seek one. She longed for a life of scholarly pursuits and art where she would not have to deal with the difficulties of social interactions. Where she wouldn't be pressured to marry. She had a fantasy about entering a convent, (although she was not Catholic), wearing a white nun's habit and growing nothing but white lilies, praying, studying and painting. Because she also dearly loved children, she comforted herself with the idea that she would simply enjoy being Aunt Ann to Nell's babies. Both she and Amanda often spent time helping with the ever-growing brood. Watching Nell and her husband often unable to make ends meet, while the babies kept coming, may have been part of her decision never to marry. But also, her unease with anything but platonic friendships was a strong factor. She told me that once a little boy had hung a May basket on her front door. As was the custom, he grabbed her and kissed her when she opened the door. She responded by chasing him down the street, slapping his face and throwing the May basket at him.

I didn't believe anyone had the right to kiss me but my parents. But, how awful that poor little boy must have felt, for he meant no harm. That was my terrible temper again.

Besides the pervasive awkwardness of her peer relationships, Gram spoke of at least two other incidents in her early years, which certainly added considerably to her discomfort. The first was when a friend of her father's touched her inappropriately when her parents had left the room for a moment. When she told them, they rightfully kicked the man out of the house and never scolded her. But she still felt degraded and it added one more piece to her confusion and distaste for relationships outside of her immediate family.

The second time was when she and a number of other children were working for a peddler in their neighborhood. Gram's incentive, as a little girl, was to buy something nice for her mother with her earnings. The children would go to the peddler's cellar where he would give them a bag of buttons and some cards. After they had sewed the buttons to the cards they would bring them back to be paid and get another batch. However, he would pay them only after they had allowed him to fondle them. I don't know how long she endured this, but she always spoke of it with sadness and hurt in her voice.

These unfortunate incidents simply added to the load of negativity in social settings that Annie seemed to encounter everywhere, except at home. All of her school years, where essential social skills must be learned, were fraught with rejection and ridicule by her peers and isolation because of her exceptional academic abilities. No doubt she was socially awkward, perhaps inadvertently appearing to feel superior. There were no accommodations for gifted students in those times, any more than for those with learning challenges. There were no school counselors to advise. Her teachers and parents were simply very proud of her. But Annie was never to be truly comfortable in social situations. Now that she was grown, Amanda and Nell both realized she did not have many friends. One thing they thought might help would be for her to dress more fashionably. That meant in the style of Charles Dana Gibson's idealized beauties. Tight corsets for impossible wasp waists, long skirts that sometimes hobbled one at the ankles, shoes that pinched the feet to make them look tiny, hair frizzed around the face, or combed over a device called a 'rat,' which built volume. Exaggerated broad brimmed hats with feather boas. Of course, Annie would have none of this. She insisted on sensible shoes, plain dresses, and once, in a fit of exasperation, tore the brim right off a hat Amanda had bought her, as the wind kept blowing it into her face. She wore her thick auburn hair in a pug all her life and eschewed rouge and powder. Any lament by her mother or Nell that she would never find a beau, was useless. She declared that she intended to be a spinster. Her thoughts on marriage are clear in this impassioned statement written about this time.

If my observations are true then there is no other one factor which enters into human society responsible for so much misery....the more holy the name the greater the profanity. The height and possible beauty of the custom may be measured by the depth of degradation to which it has fallen...we sometimes hear of 'doing evil that good may come.' An impossibility! Marriage is that custom or relation which has for its object the mutual improvement of two individuals of opposite sex, and the progression of the race toward a fuller realization of the ideal.

First she argues that marriage is the primary source of misery, and then says that it is the way to our perfection as a species. I don't know what degradation she had witnessed that moved her to write this. I do recognize Amanda's poorly advised comment about 'doing evil that good may come.' Evidently, Annie had decided that it was not true. But, this kind of lofty idealism was how she approached things. She relied on intellectual reasoning with no personal experience to test her ideas. And I believe this left her unprepared for much of life's unideal realities.

That was Annie, 23, about to graduate from art school at the top of her class. She would no longer be driving herself to exhaustion by traveling back and forth to Boston, but happily teaching art to children she loved in Abington and its surrounding towns. At home she would care for her mother, help her sister with her children, read classical literature, attend interesting lectures and concerts, and on occasion, visit her favorite cousins. It seems she had abandoned the idea of entering the convent. No one, especially Annie, could have predicted that nearly all of her intentions were about to be derailed.

chapter three

Stranger than fiction

It was the last class on a Friday before a three-day Spring break at the art school. A life drawing session, where the school provided a nude male or female model for students to learn to draw the human form.

Annie set up her easel, taped a fresh paper on it, took out some sharpened pencils and turned toward the platform where the model stood. The young man, wearing only a loincloth, was well muscled, handsome, with blue eyes and soft brown hair. This is the way my grandmother described the moment.

As I looked at him the first time I became terribly flustered. I had the unshakable feeling that somehow I knew him, when I was positive that I didn't. Even more disturbing, was the feeling that I 'belonged' to him. I had to force myself to keep looking up at him and make my drawing. As soon as the class was over I put my things away quickly, eager to get out of the room. Still standing on the platform, he spoke to my classmate.

'Excuse me, Miss, would you please be so kind as to get me a glass of water?'

She turned to me and said, 'Oh, Annie could you do that? I'm afraid I'll miss my train.'

I groaned inside. But what could I do, but bring him the glass of water? I was unable to look in his face and my hand was shaking.

'Thank you,' he said, 'Miss—?'

'...Benson,' I said, clutching my portfolio and hurrying out of the room before he could say anything else. But that was not the end of it. All the way home, on the train, I told myself that my strange feeling of knowing him, belonging to him, was because I was out of my mind with fatigue. A good rest would bring me to my senses.

Then on my first night at home I had a dream. In it, there was a letter from *him* pinned to the lower left hand corner of the bulletin board at school. I awoke in the morning disturbed that I was still thinking about him. But on the next night I had the same dream and again on the third night. By now I was feeling a bit scared and even thought I might be having a nervous breakdown.

I told Mother that only upon returning to school and seeing no letter from him on the board, would I finally be cured. So, on Tuesday morning I marched into the foyer of the school, lugging my portfolio full of completed assignments. I decided not to look at the bulletin board. I wanted my life back. I would not indulge in this insanity a moment longer. I walked right by, eyes straight ahead and started down to my locker.

'Look at the board. It's in the lower left hand corner,' said a voice in my head.

'I shan't do any such thing!' I said to myself. 'There is no letter there.' I continued downstairs, but the voice insisted. 'You must look. It is there!'

'Alright!' I responded. 'I will go back and look just to end this whole thing.'

Indeed, there was no letter where my dream had indicated. Instead there was pinned a large manila envelope addressed to someone else. Highly relieved, I thought, 'There now. That settles it once and for all,' and continued down the stairs, this time feeling triumphant to have vanquished the insistent voice. But, halfway down the stairs, I heard, 'It's under the manila envelope!' By now, quite sure of myself and not just a little angry, I marched back to the board and lifted the manila envelope. And, to my amazement, there was the letter, just as I had dreamed it, addressed to me in a fine hand. I cannot explain how my dream predicted this, but I accepted it as a true event. I sat down on the stairs and opened the envelope.

Boston, April 15, 1904

Dear Miss Benson,

If it is no inconvenience to you please meet me tomorrow (Sat) at 2:15 o'clock in the delivery room of the Public Library. It is a beautiful morning and I hope it finds you in good spirits. I am glad to see spring asserting itself. It gives one such endless opportunities to come in touch with Nature. I am fond of roaming in the summer through the fields and woods and finding a nice, comfortable place to recline, and with my book at hand pass away the hours of a pleasant day. 'Tis not time wasted for amid such surroundings one can study with hardly a conscious effort. We can then realize more fully the Omnipotence of Mind as we are the Principle, making Itself manifest so beautifully through the many varieties of vegetation. I will close this note hoping to see you soon.

Sincerely yours,
Louis R. Müller

Of course, she was stunned, and again thrown into that state of mind where none of her familiar landmarks existed. A total stranger, whose presence had radically disturbed the balance of her days, was now insisting on becoming a reality to her. Not a mere flash or a dream, but someone who wanted to know her. And from his musings about nature and spirit in this invitation, Louis seems to want her to know him as well. In fact, had Annie been more familiar with men, she might have recognized a thinly masked seduction in Louis's invitation. I believe she had no conscious intention of entering into an intimate relationship with this stranger. Nor did she interpret her feelings as 'falling in love.'

The Saturday in question had passed. He had waited and she had not appeared. She thought it only proper to explain that she had not received his note until Tuesday. So, when he was assigned as model for the life class again, she approached him, flustered, but determined to be courteous. And her courtesy was rewarded with further invitations to meet, to walk, to talk of lofty things, to correspond, perhaps to 'recline in a comfortable place in the woods' with him?

Who was this very handsome stranger? Who was he that Annie would receive him after all her pronouncements about spinsterhood and nunneries and the ubiquitous misery of marriage?

Had she actually been able to attend Bates, I can easily imagine her becoming a professor herself. And barring that, marrying someone like Professor Leakey, tramping through Greek and Egyptian ruins, writing tomes on ancient civilizations with him. Surely she would have declined a proposal from anyone without education in scholarly things. But then, I must remember that falling in love renders most of us incapable of logic.

If Gram had decided to find a mate whose beginnings and experiences were radically different from hers, then Louis would have been just right. Where she had had two devoted parents, Louis had been abandoned by his father, a sea-captain. His mother,

Mary Levinia was a lovely young minister's daughter from Halifax, Nova Scotia. After marrying the charming Captain Charles Müller and sailing to Boston with him, they settled in some rooms near the waterfront in East Boston. Charles's vessel carried cargo between Boston and Halifax and he soon was gone, leaving her pregnant. Although he promised to send money and return soon, he did neither. After several months with no word from him, Mary Levinia had to take a job as seamstress in a nearby shirt factory to pay for her rooms and buy food.

Among the families living around her was Susie, a girl of eight. Susie had had both her hearing and sight damaged by a severe case of Scarlet Fever when very young. She was not sent to school and was teased by the other children who found her odd looking. Her mother had abandoned her and various people took her in as a servant, often mistreating her. Worst of all, this pathetic little girl was actually the illegitimate daughter of Captain Charles. When Mary Levinia discovered this she was already outraged by his careless abandonment of her, and now further outraged by the abuse that Susie suffered. So she essentially adopted the girl, telling her she would now always have a home. When her baby son, Louis, was born, she placed him in Susie's care in order to return to the factory.

Many months later, Charles returned to Boston, expecting a warm welcome from his new wife. Instead, he found a mad hornet. She told him that he was no longer welcome as her husband, but that she would never divorce him. So, Louis and Susie both experienced their father on his infrequent visits, as a man always trying to ingratiate himself back into the marriage bed, but still not offering anything in return. Nevertheless, Charles and Mary Levinia maintained a strained but civil acquaintance all their lives. Louis somehow found a way to call him Father, but certainly did not have any decent model for being a husband or father himself. Without much guidance, Louis wandered the waterfront of East

Boston, learning the ways of street children, making himself useful as errand boy and later, stevedore. It was this work that had developed his fine physique, in fact. Beyond learning to read and write, he had received little schooling, nor had he learned a trade. He also did his share of drinking and carousing with women.

But, in his early twenties he had come in contact with the doctrines of Christian Science, which greatly appealed to him. He became a teetotaler and was an ardent, even zealous convert and found fellow believers at the Mother Church in Boston.

Annie had met him just at this turning point, where he was struggling to redefine himself, to reach higher. They were both moving toward new concepts. She had to justify pursuing a relationship that was not platonic. He had to believe he was worthy of a refined, educated, competent, virginal woman. She had to believe that he was capable of overcoming his flaws and needed only her unfailing love and help to do so. When he tried to tell her that he was not good enough for her, she would hear none of it. During their courtship he writes—

> *Dear Annie, Your virtue rebukes my sensuality. It seems like selfishness in me to claim your friendship when I find so little that is really good in me to offer you for it. I feel sometimes that I am two persons. Louis*

She answers—

> *Dear Louis, You speak of this other Louis who seems inclined to get between you and me. Well, I've never seen him, and if I did I should find him disgusting and intolerable because he is the most deadly enemy of my very dear friend, L.R.M. I hope that someday there shall be only one of you, the friend I value now. Annie*

They discussed marriage quite early in their relationship. Annie, the determined spinster, now wore a delicate gold engagement ring with five fire-opals. And eventually there were embraces and kisses that did not receive a slap in the face, as this excerpt from one of her letters reveals.

> ....*Yes, my love for you is great, its limits are the limits of my nature, and as I grow my love for you must grow in proportion. Deserve such love? You deserve the best I have to give, and more, you know that those things in your life which might seem to stand between us were and are not any part of you. Time shall prove that the man I love and honor, who receives my most sincere respect is the only real man. It shall prove to those (if there be any) who think differently that I have seen and known you, they have 'seen through a glass' darkened and overspread by the unrealities which conceal the truth. The same feeling of loving trust and security that I felt with my dear father comes to me within those strong arms, and the pleasantness of lips in mutual expression of joy at our nearness to each other is unalloyed by any sense of shame. The lips I kiss are as pure as my own though the whole Decalogue of sins should try to testify to the contrary, I should say to them, 'I do not know you.' They say love has the power to cast out devils, and I know it. Unwavering Love may walk through the valley of Death and fear no evil.*
> *Your Annie Belle B.*

Although Christian Science was a hopeful and positive beacon for Louis, he was somewhat fanatical in his interpretations. And he was as eager to instruct her as she was to instruct him. To win every disagreement, he quoted Mary Baker Eddy with the burning fervor of a new convert. He was not interested in reading classics. He preferred the Christian Science Bible, *Science and Health*, or meeting with other Scientists. Instead of learned lectures he sought exhibitions of people like The Great Houdini, and Sandow, a popular figure in the world of physical culture. He entered contests of male body-builders, wrestling matches, ate radical diets of nature foods, belonged to a cycling group and did long-distance ocean swimming feats. And his devoted Annie bravely tried to share his interests. She ate raw oats, got eaten alive by mosquitoes on camping and hiking trips, designed and lovingly embroidered his monogram on his exhibition shirt. She tried and tried to understand Mary Baker Eddy's theories, even though she had never embraced any one set of ideas or religious denomination. Rather, she loved to study and challenge all systems that claimed to contain the Truth. But she respected his interests and tried very hard to join him at the lectures and exhibitions that so excited him, even though they were quite unsettling to her. She did not share his admiration of men who attracted attention to themselves through physical prowess. She admired great thinkers, men of high ideals and brilliance, poets and philosophers. Men like Socrates or Emerson—didn't care if they were dwarves or had puny muscles. Still she did speak glowingly of Louis's magnificent body and handsome face, a fact in her attraction to him that she never was able to own. She was so confident that dear Louis needed only to be encouraged to believe in himself as she did. And she also thought that by sharing her love of learning, she could bridge the gap between their worlds. Her enthusiasm and idealism were undaunted.

It is not clear when they decided to move in together, but before they married, they managed to buy two adjacent houses in Malden, Massachusetts, a pleasant small city north of Boston. They intended to rent out the second house for income. They, and their two widowed mothers all moved in together. Amanda and Mary Levinia each had an attic bedroom. There were two more large bedrooms on the second floor, one connected to a small room that would be used as nursery. Another room would serve as library/studio for Annie. Downstairs were the front parlor with French doors into an ample dining room, and a kitchen with pantry. Their back yard rose to a terrace that Annie planted with many iris, lilies and spring bulbs. Eventually there would be an arbor for roses, a mulberry tree full of birds, and a fragrant grapevine, with a Linden tree for shade. Nearby was a public park with a lovely pond surrounded by willow trees.

True to form, Annie had no desire for a fancy wedding dress, or to spend precious money on a wedding trip. So, one ordinary March day, they went to city hall and had a civil marriage. She wore her plain gold ring for the rest of her life- the only authentic jewelry she ever owned, besides her opal engagement ring.

Annie now had to resign from her job as art supervisor in the Abingtons, as married women were not allowed to teach, or even be librarians. She and Louis began attending a Christian Science Church in Malden, the largest one in Massachusetts besides the Mother Church in Boston. After a short period Louis was elected as First Reader. First Reader is an honorable position in place of minister, and he won 95 of 128 votes. His acceptance speech was heartfelt gratitude. In a letter to his mother he thanks his beloved Annie for believing in him, and states that this appointment will move him toward 'true manhood.' Louis was also studying to become a practitioner, which would allow him to charge 'patients' for healing prayer sessions. He would use their front parlor for his practice.

Quite often Amanda took the train to Abington to visit Nell and help with the babies. Consequently Annie wrote many letters to her that describe her daily life in 1906.

Dearest Mother,
I had intended to write a long letter but have been slow.
Lots of good news.

Louis' income for this week is $41.00. I am getting along well with my work and have a contract for a steady $24.00 monthly for my watercolor miniatures.

Today I made1 cheap fruit cake, 1 golden loaf, 1 Lilly cake, 1 qt. beans, rhubarb sauce, boiled 5 lbs of neck, swept my front hall, bedroom, dining room, dusted all, washed kitchen floor, watered lawns and gardens, ironed 2 bed spreads, 2 dresses, 2 petties, shirt, collar band, flannel jacket, hankies, etc., made all meals and did the dishes. All on Saturday.

Will write a decent letter tomorrow. So good night.

Nan (her mother's pet name for her)

Things seemed to be going well. Louis was well liked at church. He began to have a few patients. But he had done something that would cost him and Annie dearly.

Captain Charles was now retired from the sea and living in New York at Safe Harbor, a home for old sailors. He received a pension for his years at sea and Louis had gone to New York to talk to his father about this pension. Louis had a friend who was a lawyer. His friend suggested that Charles's pension could be invested and vastly increased. So, Louis convinced his father to give him the money to be invested by his friend. Unfortunately, Louis's lawyer friend managed to lose the money and Charles never saw a penny of his pension again. His requests to have the money returned were unanswered. Naturally he was upset and complained bitterly to his devoted sister, Julia. Perhaps she had expected to receive a share of this pension upon his death, because she was outraged. She wrote several strong letters to her nephew, Louis, castigating him for 'robbing' an old man, leaving him destitute. This was not true, as Charles had a comfortable berth and had willingly given Louis the money. But it was true that Louis had not been able to keep his promise. He did not have the ability to judge people's motives and make wise decisions at all. In any case, when Aunt Julia got no response from Louis, she threatened to come to his church during a service and tell them that their First Reader had stolen his father's pension and left him penniless. And now he was standing up there pretending to be a righteous and holy person, she would say. She kept her promise.

When the church elders heard her accusations, Louis was summarily dismissed. Sadly, that would be the first and last steady employment that he would ever have. Now he had no job, and a bad public reputation in the community to boot. Even more poignant, his standing in the church, which was so essential to his goal for self-improvement, was greatly damaged. But there was even more to come.

Shortly after the terrible pension fiasco, Annie was busy painting in her studio when the doorbell rang. Annie answered it and found a young, pregnant woman standing on the porch.

"Does Louis Müller live here?" asked the woman.

"Why, yes," said Annie, thinking that the woman might be one of Louis's patients.

"Well, you tell him that I am carrying his baby," said the woman. "And tell him if he doesn't keep his promise and marry me, I will kill myself." She turned and went to the sidewalk. "And tell him I'm staying at the hotel," she called back before walking away.

When Louis returned, Annie confronted him. He denied any knowledge of the pregnant woman. Although she never came back, the damage was done.

I am sure there were many tears and long, hot conversations after both these events. Many wives would have been embittered. In fact, some may have summarily decided that he was not worth it. Whatever Annie felt, though, she believed that marriage was forever. She put on a brave face and carried on. Incredibly, she was still convinced that he was truly a beautiful soul just needing her love and support.

In his behalf, he could be very endearing. The hint of promise went a long way. The possibility of that summer day reclining in some beautiful glen, sharing a lofty book together and discussing the creation kept her hoping. She was in love with what he might be, rather than what he actually was able to be. He also had a knack of gifting her with sensitivity, like his wedding gift. He had bought her a marble bust of a Grecian beauty and told her it looked like her. And after every fall his abject self-criticism was very touching. The loss of his position in the church must have been devastating to him, especially since his self-esteem already suffered. In a letter to his mother, he wrote of his shame and disappointment in himself. But more importantly, he said he was sorry not to be worthy of his beloved Annie.

But why did he trust the lawyer's glib promises with his father's life savings? I do know that he was always looking for the pot of gold. In spite of his rough upbringing he was not really worldly-wise. He had no training or skills that made him suitable for any conventional employment. Instead, he saw himself as one of those lucky ones who would stumble upon a get-rich-quick scheme. He was not alone, for that was actually the Zeitgeist of the early 1900s

In the meantime he did manage to make a little money with little effort. A few of his patients stayed with him in spite of his demotion. And because he had rare Type O blood, he was a regular paid donor at Massachusetts General Hospital. Infrequently, he posed for magazine ads, perhaps modeling for some new shaving cream, his face covered with lather. He entered wrestling contests and male physique exhibitions, but rarely won much.

Then there were his inventions. The waterproof shopping bag with a varnished bottom that would not break when soaked. One could set it down on a rainy day at the bus stop, and the oranges would not roll out on the sidewalk when you picked it up. An improved in oil-burner ring for stoves newly converted from coal and wood. All natural honey ginger ale. Delicious raisin candy made with almonds, lemon juice and fresh coconut. Alfalfa/ lemon sherbet. All but the sherbet might have been successful. Annie would design a tasteful logo printed with his name as President of the company. Then the whole effort would come to a screeching halt. No one could convince him to let someone else market his product. And since he didn't know how to manage such things at all, many stillborn prototypes ended up in the cellar. A sad testimony to his tragic stubbornness and a lifetime of failed schemes.

Annie had to work her mind around all this and continue believing in him. In her letters to her sister, Annie put on a brave front, exalting Louis's efforts as though they were just about to go on the market. He even bought a car that he said just needed a little work. When his inventions sold he would get it fixed. The poor car quietly sank into the driveway as tires rotted and fenders rusted away. Its corpse was visible beneath the room where Gram worked at her easel and each glance was a stinging reminder of all Louis's unfulfilled promises. But he would not allow the car to be towed away. Rather, he would surprise her with a mahogany music box, beautifully crafted and able to play twelve tunes like a mellow harp. And she would see the beauty in his heart instead of his faulty thinking.

Graduation from teacher's college,
Annie at 21

Annie just married, March, 1906

Louis, 28 in shirt with Annie's
monogram

chapter four
The changeling

It was two years after their marriage that Annie became pregnant. They were happy. Louis was sure they would have a son. His name would be Carl Müller. He was so sure, he went to the printer and had cards made up to hand out to his friends at the athletic club. Springtime came, and on May 18, 1908, a beautiful baby girl was born. Annie was thrilled. But Louis wasn't. He would not even enter the bedroom to see the child. What was he to tell his friends? What use were the birth announcement cards? It was her error in thinking that had caused this, he said. Annie's heart was nearly broken. I don't know how many days passed before he came into the room to see his daughter. It is not that every marriage doesn't have its imperfections, especially in the early years, but surely this incident added to the list of hurtful actions and left a deep scar.

And now they had to find a girl's name they could agree on. First, Louis made the outrageous suggestion that they name her Maud Kranz Müller. Maud Kranz was a nurse he had once known and loved. He had hoped to marry her, but she died. (Hadn't anyone ever told him not to talk about his old loves, especially when naming his first baby?) Of course Annie bridled at the idea, but rather than castigate him for this, she patiently persuaded him that it was a poor choice because of a popular poem at that time, about a girl named Maud Müller. In the poem, Maud Müller is a poor farm girl who 'on a summer's day, rakes the meadow sweet with hay...' when a wealthy judge stops his horse and asks for a cup of water. They converse and part. Each one unhappily marries someone from their own station in life, but is left dreaming of the other still. It is the poem, by John Greenleaf Whittier in which the line, "...for all sad words of tongue or pen, the saddest are these: it might have been!" Gram argued that she did not want her daughter to be associated with the unfortunate life of this farm lass. I wonder also if she saw a little of herself in Maud's unfortunate marriage. In any case, they compromised. Gram chose Irene, which means 'peace' in Greek. She allowed the middle name to be Kranz. Irene Kranz Müller, it was.

Eventually, Louis was able to accept his little girl and became quite affectionate, taking her for walks around the pond, and holding her on his lap for pictures. He bought her a baby bunny and built a hutch for it. Later on, he would teach her to be a strong swimmer like himself. But, as a very young child, she was often very ill.

Annie had been raised to use natural remedies whenever possible, and to call a trusted physician if things didn't improve. Louis was deeply convinced that the sincere practice of Christian Science ensured perfect health. I wish to make it clear that I am not in any way qualified to speak of the thinking of all Christian Scientists, and in no way seek to discredit their beliefs. Rather, I am writing about how these disparate approaches to health caused great distress for Annie and Louis, and their child.

Annie had found a doctor who was respectful of her home remedies, but was also ready to step in with medical advice and treatment when she became alarmed or anxious. Louis could see no use for medical consultation even when the baby had been ill for days, was losing weight, crying, and sometimes passing blood with an intestinal infection. Annie would overrule him. Dr. Burpee would come and prescribe the mildest of remedies and Irene would improve. Then she would become sick again because unbeknownst to Annie, or the doctor, Louis had decided to feed her some natural grain cereal he had mixed. Then they would have a huge argument with her telling him that he had nearly killed their baby and him telling her that it was her negative thinking that was keeping the baby ill. Hardly an atmosphere for healing, even though both Annie and Louis were sincerely worried and trying to keep their child well. I believe that any child who knows it is the subject of parental quarrels may feel unsafe and that they are at fault. And, indeed my mother's early memories confirm this. She remembered heated discussions over her treatment when she was sick in bed. Gram bringing in Dr. Burpee when Louis was not home. Grampa coaxing her to eat his nature food recipes when Grama was busy elsewhere. Once, when she was about four, she remembered being so weak she had to crawl up the stairs. Gram paid for ballet lessons, suggested by Dr. Burpee, to strengthen her legs.

But, Irene also had everything her parents could think of to make her happy. Even with little money to spare, there was Tom kitten, and a small dog, Skippy, Peep, the canary and Peter the bunny. She wore hand-made middy blouses made of the finest soft wool, pretty hair ribbons, shiny patent leather shoes. She had beautifully illustrated storybooks and walks around the pond with one or the other of her kind grandmothers. Gram organized a croquet club, made up an official brochure and logo with news of games. The neighborhood children would gather in Irene's spacious, grassy backyard to play. That way, Annie could see from her studio window that Irene was safe. For her tenth birthday, Annie sewed Japanese costumes for her and several friends, made tiny shrimp sandwiches and very weak tea with honey. She bought each girl a paper parasol and hung lanterns on the porch for them to have their Japanese tea party.

In spite of needing to be at her easel for hours daily, Annie would always find time to provide this kind of experience for her child. If she neglected anything it was housekeeping and that troubled her a great deal. She was able to hire a helper sometimes, but was overwhelmed by nine rooms and the expectation of four other people to keep order, prepare meals and provide income for all of them. Her preference was showing Irene how to make a miniature landscape in a tray of sand, with a tiny glass swan floating across a lake made from a pocket mirror, bits of dried moss for shrubs. Or on a drizzly day, to make molasses popcorn balls in the cozy kitchen. She was never the distant mother, but more like a Mary Poppins Nanny, eager to play, to provide, teach, laugh, explore. And the housework piled up and up, always nagging her conscience. She really believed that she was supposed to do it all.

Over the years Mary Levinia had suffered from "melancholia," now called depression. So Annie would coax her out of her room to take Irene for a walk. Her mother-in-law was yet another person whose happiness she was responsible for. Perhaps she identified a little with Mary Levinia's unhappy marriage? In any case, when Irene was three, Mary Levinia died, and it was Annie who cared tenderly for her.

Seven years later Grandmother Amanda contracted pneumonia. Annie was resigned to the fact that her mother might not survive at the age of 78. And though she tended her lovingly night and day, she could see she was failing.

Neither when his own mother was dying nor at this time was Louis able to be of help. His mind, set on healing and health, denied the reality of illness and death. So, he chose this crucial time to take an interesting trip. He knew that his father's grandfather was a German Jewish immigrant who had made a great deal of money. He had lived and died in Philadelphia. Louis decided to see if he could find any other relatives and perhaps some property entitlements for himself from this great-grandfather. So, rather than support Annie during her mother's last illness, he decided to go to Philadelphia to tend to this important business. And he would swing by Niagara Falls on the way home. She begged him not to leave her alone, but he went anyway.

When her beloved mother died there was no one there to comfort Annie. All she got from her Louis was a post card of the Falls, telling her what a great time he was having. I think she could no longer explain or justify Louis's actions to herself by now. They were so contrary to any reasonable expectation of husbandly responsibility. Surely, even a good friend might have been more supportive. Added to the disgrace of the poorly conceived scheme regarding his father's pension and that awful scene with the pregnant woman at the front door, dismissal as First Reader, his insistence on her participating in all his interests, but not reciprocating and his bizarre response to Irene's birth, Annie had little to support her original faith in him. She was married, but at great cost and little benefit, if any, it seems. There was also the humiliation of knowing that others could see these glaring flaws. Her neighbor's husbands went to work in Boston each day. Even more painful, she knew that her mother and Nell did not think much of Louis. And her own beliefs were being so sorely tested. To realize how great her fall from hope was, one need only to read part of a letter she wrote to him just before they had married.

> *Just think what an opportunity is awaiting me! To bring more brightness into three lives, yours and our mothers; if I am only good enough. Just the simple everyday virtues like kindness, cheerfulness, sweet temper, self-forgetfulness are within my reach if I will but put out my hand to receive them—fame is not their accompaniment but you sent me long ago a little poem which rings true, 'such a life tho, it were to find no other channel for its activities would bring that content that only comes to sinless days and innocent; a life devoid of fame or praise yet nobly spent.'*
>
> *What a glorious little haven our home shall be! A quiet little harbor so surrounded by 'the hills from which cometh our strength' that we may find calmness and shelter there from*

all storms. A place in which, surrounded by the simple joys
of common life we may take council together about all things,
and where we both know there is one who knows our real self.
A little 'Holy of Holies' into which we may enter at will, and
shutting out the noise of the crowd, listen to that 'Harmony
which never really ceases' and so go forth again among men
with it still ringing in our ears above the din of Babel.
    With the fullest measure of love.
    Annie Belle B.

What strikes me in this letter is the fact that she says, at the beginning, that she will have the opportunity to make three people happy. Where is the fourth person: herself? She sees everyone else's happiness as her responsibility, if only she can be virtuous enough. So, when they are not happy, it must be a fault in her. She sees selflessness as ignoring her own needs, which allows everyone else to take advantage without any return. And I cringe when she says their life will be completely free from storms. I want to counsel this dear young woman and save her from the inevitable pain she will suffer, the terrible dénouement. But then, she was young and in love. And her Louis proclaimed his love as well.

Of course, isn't all young love dangerously naïve? It's just that most of us don't leave such a detailed written record to be judged by our descendants. Even though she told me many things, both happy and sad, about her life, I try to remember that I wasn't there. My critique comes from the long view. That is, knowing how she and Louis were as an older couple. Knowing what became of Irene. Knowing what Gram, herself, spoke of in her last years as failed efforts; her voice sad and bewildered rather than blameful.

According to my mother, there were times that Annie was very distracted and distressed by her marital problems. She was often painting late into the night to meet a deadline, and consequently exhausted next day. She cried a lot, sometimes even neglecting to make meals. My mother claimed that she was once hungry enough to try to dig up beets and carrots from the neighbor's garden to feed herself. I find this hard to believe and Gram denied that it ever happened, yet it might have been. For in her later years Gram told me that there had been several times when she was so discouraged that she had imagined how nice it would be to slip under the waters of the pond and simply drown herself. She reported being struck by a car twice during those years, with minor injuries, due to inattention while crossing the street. She may have been less attentive if she were very depressed. I am thankful that she did not believe in suicide. Instead she soldiered on, trying to do right.

It was also during this time that she had a nearly fatal fall at home. She was painting, when the little dog, Skippy, needed to go out. Annie got up in haste and hurrying down stairs, tripped and fell to the bottom.

> Next thing, I was standing up over a prone, moaning body on the floor. I was astonished to see that it was I, lying in a pool of blood. I thought, 'Oh, dear. More trouble for Louis.' Then I found myself on the front porch of our neighbor, Mrs. Thorpe.
>
> I rang the bell and she opened her door. 'Oh, Mrs. Müller!' she said. 'What happened? You're hurt.' I knew nothing until the next day. I had fractured my skull and needed to lie flat for quite some time. But what interests me is how I walked to Mrs. Thorpe's in that condition, when I couldn't walk for weeks afterward. And how was I able to stand over 'myself' lying on the floor?

Gram was always interested in psychic phenomena and read a great deal about paranormal experiences. In her later life, she sent this episode in to a group of researchers at Duke University. They included it in a research book on out-of-body experiences.

But with all these disasters she still had secured a contract with Rust Craft Greeting Card Co., which was the leading company of its kind in New England then. She would write to various publishers about her work, get an appointment to bring in samples and literally convince them to commission her, bargaining for a decent return. Now she was painting babies as well as floral scenes, being paid more and working longer hours.

Beacon Academy, a Christian Science high school near Boston hired her to teach art. She arranged to have Irene sit as a model. And later, Irene also had an after-school job working in the office of an Ophthalmologist. He was a kind man, and enjoyed teaching her medical things, which greatly interested her. This interest, no doubt, was fired by her early illnesses and the conflicts around them. So small streams of money kept them afloat, with Annie becoming more and more successful. Boston Metropolitan Lithograph commissioned calendars with pictures of babies. One of their managers would even come to the house to look at her work. Vanta Baby Garments bought many babies she painted for advertisements.

Every bit of money that wasn't needed for coal, food or the house, was spent on the 'nicer' things of life for Irene. Annie was able to buy a good piano and hired Mrs. Thorpe's daughter, a student at New England Conservatory, to be Irene's teacher. Irene was very talented and continued lessons through high school, playing Chopin Nocturnes, Rachmaninoff and even Gershwin's *Rhapsody in Blue*, beautifully. When given a chance to sing in a school production a local newspaper reported that 'Irene Müller is a star.'

Annie made sure that her daughter would know about all the beautiful things that a cultured young lady could enjoy; all the things she, herself, had never known. She even enrolled Irene in a social club that embraced only young ladies from the West Side of town.

But Irene was no longer a little girl. She was becoming her own person, no longer kept to the yard under her mother's watchful eye. She used to walk to the streetcar stop and sit on the wall to watch all the fathers coming home from work in Boston; all but hers. They carried important briefcases that she imagined contained money. She wondered how they got the money, because money was very often a topic at home. Like many children in their early teens she developed an opinion that her parents were peculiar. And they were quite different, in that her mother worked, her father didn't and they rarely socialized. Being an only child, Irene did not have the opportunity to compare her impressions with siblings. She was imaginative and bright, observed carefully, but often drew inaccurate conclusions. All children do this, but she did it to the extreme, even fabricating at times. For Annie, who revered truth, this was anathema. But, the more she lectured her daughter, the more Irene retreated into her own version of things.

Irene was an early bloomer and by the time she was a freshman, she was physically mature and very beautiful. She and her mother were no longer confidantes. Irene kept up a façade, but did as she pleased. She thought school was quite boring, but still attended and would do well enough to be accepted at college later. She spent a great deal of time reading through the library stacks on subjects she enjoyed, such as Irish mythology and modern history. Rather than the West Side girls club, she preferred visiting the homes of classmates who lived on the East Side of town with their immigrant parents—Italians, Irish, Jews who spoke little English. Their houses were small and shabby, with yards full of grapevines, chicken coops, tomato plants and pigpens. Their food was savory and intriguing. They drank wine, which was considered an evil in her abstinent home. (Louis would not even allow her to eat Rum Raisin ice cream, although it had no alcohol in it.) The Irish and Italian families were Catholic, had statues of the Madonna in their parlors and said their rosaries.

I'm sorry to say that both Annie and Louis considered Catholicism an alien, inferior religion. This was rooted in the fact that both of them had grown up in predominantly Protestant New England, and the insurgence of Catholic immigrants was uncomfortable for many at that time. Stories about priests, nuns and their babies were told as though common fact. My high-minded grandmother thought Catholics did not think for themselves. She was very proud of her colonial roots and felt superior to more recent immigrants, though I am sure she would have denied it. But her bias took shape in comments about the Italian fruit peddler with rosy cheeks, who was so charmed by Irene that he always gave her a free apple. Even as a child I got the idea that she thought he was a simpleton. She sang a little ditty about the Irish: "They kept the pig in the parlor, and he was Irish too." All very funny, yet demeaning. When pregnant with Irene she had hired an African-American woman as maid. The woman was also pregnant. Both babies arrived at about the same time. Some weeks later the maid came back to work. Gram told me of this exchange between them.

"How is your new baby?" asked Annie

"She died." the maid answered.

"Oh, dear, how terrible. I'm so sorry," said Annie.

"Easy come, easy go." said the maid, flatly.

Gram told me this story more than once. Each time she said she could not imagine being so callous about the death of one's child, especially as she had just given birth herself, and adored her baby. She did not consider that the maid might have had very different circumstances around her pregnancy—poverty, perhaps had been raped, perhaps had twelve children already, perhaps could not bear to speak of it to Mrs. White Lady. So, from that story, as a child, I drew the conclusion that only white people loved their babies. From the ditty about the Irish pig in the parlor, I thought that Irish people were dirty. Not refined like us.

It was years before I even realized that I had been inoculated with these biases, and am grateful that I no longer make such negative assumptions about others. But, what it illustrates is the possibility that my mother might have been testing these same biases against her own experience on the other side of town. Irene's strong attraction to this other world is understandable. Not just because she knew her parents did not approve of 'foreigners,' but because she saw cohesive, earthy, family life there. For better or worse, these immigrant families worked together to survive and thrive in their new world. They had little time for pretense. And sadly, she had seen too much of that at home. Annie always erecting a brave front while Louis was just about to start a business, or discover a splendid scheme, when actually he did nothing but absent treatments for patients he claimed he had. That entailed sitting in the front parlor with his eyes closed. He had even begun putting on his only suit each morning, and leaving the house. He said he was 'going to business.' Then he would get on the trolley and disappear into Boston until evening, sometimes bringing home a small gift for Irene, a fountain pen, or new hairbrush for Annie. But never a paycheck.

So the alienation of their only daughter was woven into the fabric of their own parenting, subtle and silent and totally contrary to what they hoped for her. In spite of Annie's best efforts to raise Irene with a desire for classical education and culture, and Louis's desire for her to embrace Christian Science, Irene wanted none of it. She practiced her classical music, but loved the new thing called jazz, too, which distressed her parents, rather typical for someone entering adolescence. But Irene's rebellion was as extreme as her parents' restrictions had been. The only written record of the family dynamic at this period are some letters written when Irene was sixteen. She and her mother stayed at a cottage on a saltwater cove in Bath, Maine. Louis was to join them at some point, but for some reason remained in Malden.

A small cloud of anxiety about Irene's attractiveness to the local boys is visible behind Annie's report in a letter to Louis from Bath.

Clarence went swimming with Irene last week and had an asthma attack and insists that he owes his life to Irene who swam to him and took him up on shore while Ed ran for a kind of inhaler that he has to use in severe attacks. I told his mother how sorry we were for encouraging him to go into the water, but she doesn't blame us at all. She laughed and said, "I'm going to tell you what everyone says. They say the young lady at the cottage doesn't have much chance to be lonesome because Ed and Clarence take turns seeing to it that she isn't." She seems to like Irene and so does everyone else if we can judge at all by the way we are treated. Clarence's father brought us a fresh cod fish and green beans from his garden yesterday and I had to insist on giving him a quarter for it. That will be a delicious supper tonight with the raspberries we picked.

I visited Miss Coombs and she said that her little son Louis talks about Irene all the time. He told her how Irene rows and swims and dives and turns somersaults in the water and how nice she looks. But he says she ought to see Irene when she gets dressed up in her knickerbockers. "She's a corker!"

It isn't Irene's fault exactly, do you think, that Ed and Clarence are in competition to keep her entertained? Irene does nothing to make herself up. Her only powder is the dried salt left on her skin from swimming in the cove. This is the first summer for 3 years that I feel Irene has acted with good sense. I don't wonder the boys like to be with her and she surely has lots of fun with them and I can see nothing amiss about it. She even laughs with me about the complicated plots the boys invent to include her in their picnics, boat rides and fishing

and says she is glad it is all temporary as it would become
annoying if we lived here all the time.

In other letters, she speaks quite a bit about trying to stay fit, to lose weight and live simply. It is apparent that she and Louis have spoken extensively about these issues before, with him making up exercise routines for both Annie and Irene. Louis, himself, would fast at times and put himself on radical diets of raw foods. So Annie tries, without much conviction or success, to please him by doing situps, pushups and pullups and reporting back to him about pounds lost and inches dropped. Anyone reading her letters would see a wife clearly still in love with her husband, and with normal concerns about her daughter. And Irene seems to be enjoying her summer with her mother even though the letters say *Irene's French lessons are going very well but the Latin not so well* and *Now don't send us any more things as we want to eliminate all matter that does not contribute to our growth—like Diogenes and his tub. We have everything we need except YOU!*

Photographs show that eventually Louis did join them in Bath. It was probably there that Louis coached Irene's long-distance ocean swimming. Later, the two of them even swam in Boston Harbor together, all the way out to Egg Rock, which is at least a mile. So, it is a relief to know that there were times when they managed to have fun as a family even with such limited resources, and all the trials endured so far. And, as with all adolescents, they were parents concerned for their child's safety and success. Certainly the times of speak-easies, bobbed hair, short skirts and the Charleston danced to the jarring new music of jazz and ragtime was enough to alarm any parent. The Victorian era, with its formalities, inhibitions and secrets was over. And Irene was a true, sassy flapper. She was the 'cat's pajamas' and the 'bee's knees' with a tiny opium pipe in her pocket. And she had every new generation's utter disdain for parental mores.

Irene at two years, with her parents

Irene, 10 models at Beacon School where Annie teaches art.

Irene at 14

chapter five

Three's a crowd

Back in Malden, with Amanda gone, her empty room was rented out to a friend of Louis's who actually paid a monthly sum. This arrangement at least brought in some money, and 'Uncle' Joe, as Irene called him, became a pleasant addition to the family. Perhaps he even helped to keep the lid on various tinderboxes, as families often manage to avoid arguing around non-family members. There was still Mary Levinia's empty room. And now Louis told Annie that his half-sister, Susie would be moving in. This was not a discussion with options. It was an announcement.

When Susie was in her thirties, she had married Captain Foote, a man much older than she. Now a widow in her sixties, Susie had no one but her beloved Louis to care for her. And he felt quite responsible to do so. It might have been easier if Susie has been a pleasant person. But her early rejections had soured her. She could read and write and had very basic cooking skills. She mended clothes and was personally clean. But from the very beginning, her perception of Annie was skewed. Annie simply was not 'family.'

It would not have occurred to Annie to say Susie could not come. After all, her task was to make others happy. So on Susie's first night at their home, Annie worked very hard and made a nice roast chicken dinner. During the meal Louis asked Susie, "What do you think of Annie's cooking, Susie? Isn't this delicious?"

"It's all right… considerin'," answered Susie, flatly.

Gram remembered wondering 'considering' what? She would find out that Susie meant 'considering' that Annie was not one of their family. Considering that Susie saw herself as Louis's close relative and Annie a peripheral acquaintance of some sort.

Very soon, Louis showed that he felt similarly. "Annie, you needn't wait up for me anymore and interrupt your painting. Susie will get my meals from now on. I'll bring something home and we shall eat supper together in the kitchen."

He saw this as a thoughtful thing to do, to relieve Annie of cooking, without understanding how powerfully it separated them as man and wife. Annie saw it as him trying to be kind, that he didn't intend to hurt her. And she also knew that she could never challenge the bond that he and Susie had forged since their beginnings. So this is how their remaining years were shaped.

They still shared a bed. But for years after Irene's birth, that had not been a happy place either. Louis did not want any more children, whereas Annie would have liked at least one more. He felt that her sexual yearnings were improper, and scolded her for causing him to give in, calling it 'malicious animal magnetism,' a Christian Science term that he often misused to label something she did. And although Annie had once never wanted to marry, she had the healthy sexual appetite of a woman in love.

Louis's lack of interest in her had other implications that were not possible to mention at the time. But in her later years, Gram said out loud that she believed he was homosexual. And as a child, my observations of his male friends would bear that out. Men who smelled strongly of aromatic lotions and wore diamond rings. Men he had met in clubs in Boston, who enjoyed the steam baths. There were also numerous pictures of naked men in the attic that fascinated me as a child. When I innocently mentioned them to Gram, she wisely explained that both she and Grampa thought that the naked body was beautiful. She said that they had enjoyed nudist beaches when they were younger. She reminded me that he had been a model and body builder and that the pictures were simply some of his friends that had the same interests. I was never scolded for looking at them and decided they were interesting but not important. I give her lots of credit for handling my curiosity with such tact, so much better than her mother Amanda had been able to do for her.

To make a list of all the things awry within their marriage would seem to put Louis always at fault. But, I don't know his point of view. My grandfather never talked about her to me, nor did he really tell me much about himself. The only topic he voluntarily shared was Christian Science doctrine, or healthy foods and how to strengthen my muscles. Whereas I was able to talk to Gram about nearly everything until in my early forties; Grampa had died when I was twelve, too young to ask him what I would like to know now. That is: How did you feel being married to this brilliant, talented idealist, who expected you to morph into a Greek god under her tender tutelage? Were you drawn to men at a time when there was no acceptable way to 'come out'? Did Susie's presence provide a convenient barrier to closeness without openly divorcing? What did you do all day in Boston? How did you justify allowing your wife to be the breadwinner? Is it true that you felt like a failure? O, Grampa, what was in your heart that made you stay all that long time? Were you at all happy? Did you really love her?

All questions I can only speculate upon. And as for Annie's part in their troubles, I have just as many questions. Did she nag and lecture him a lot? Overwhelm him with her idealistic views? Or was it mainly her naïveté about men that fogged her vision when he tried to warn her of his flaws during courtship. And what kept her from sending him away? Surely after their mothers were gone, and Irene nearly grown, she could have supported herself and escaped the strange intrusion of Susie. But, women of her day did not take marriage lightly. It was truly for better or worse, till death do us part. So they stayed together with 'patience and endurance,' Gram used to say, wryly quoting from *Science and Health* text. The arrangement would endure.

Susie settled into the kitchen rocker, sipping tea, napping, reading and waiting for her brother each day. Annie painted, did laundry by hand, cooked for herself and Irene. Sometimes she had to go to Boston or New York to meet with publishers. She would devote occasional days to concerts and operas, buying Irene a seat in front rows, while she sat in the second balcony. Periodically they would visit the Boston Museum of Fine Art. In front of the museum was a statue, still there, for which Louis had been the model. It is called, "Appeal to the Great Spirit" by Cyrus Dallin, and depicts a Native American in full Western headdress sitting on his horse with arms raised. Louis posed only for the arms, torso and legs and a genuine Indian posed for the head; a metaphor for the man who was truly only partially present as husband and father.

With Susie as his main companion, Louis felt even less need to talk things over with Annie. One day as she was working upstairs, she heard him welcoming people into the house. They hardly ever entertained guests due to financial restraints as well as the intrusion on her working hours. She thought they were probably some Christian Science friends, so kept on working. Later on, she asked him who had called.

"Oh, that was my aunt and uncle from Halifax," said Louis. "Susie and I hadn't seen them for years. We had a wonderful visit."

"Why didn't you call me? I would love to have met them," said Annie. "Will they be coming by again?"

"No, they're on their way back to Nova Scotia," said Louis. "We didn't see any need to disturb you."

"After all, Annie," Susie chimed in, "They're not your relatives."

Louis obviously found this wall of exclusion preferable. So, Annie stopped protesting. And within this dynamic Irene made her observations, drew her conclusions about her parents, lived her secret life. Neither of her parents had any idea what she was thinking, or doing when away from home. They both noticed her increasing flippancy, caught her in lies, lectured her without making a dent. Besides, Louis was extra busy at this time with his grandest scheme yet.

He had met a husband and wife within his church group. They were from New Hampshire with lots of interesting things to say about a mica mine there. At that time mica was the mineral used in making a thin, transparent material called isinglass for car windows. This mine could be bought for, let's say, ten thousand dollars. Keep in mind that this was enough to buy several houses in the 1920s. Such a mine could yield hundreds of thousands eventually, as the car industry was growing fast. It sounded like the perfect opportunity for Louis to finally make his fortune. He talked to Annie.

"But Louis, you need to see the mine to make sure it is real. And you need to check the credentials of these people. Who are they? You really don't know them. It is only their word you have to go on," she said, wisely.

"Oh, Annie! They are Christian Scientists. They would never lie to me. Your mind is full of error. I trust them completely. Of course the mine is real," said exasperated Louis.

"But where are you to get ten thousand dollars?" asked Annie.

"I will present my idea to everyone we know and convince them to invest in the mine," said Louis, firmly. "That's how it's done."

With Annie still totally skeptical, he went forward with Susie right beside him. He talked to people at the church and in their neighborhood. And eventually he had enough money to present to the couple who then gave him the coveted deed to the mine. The next step was to take a trip to New Hampshire and survey his new property, or shall we say, the property in which he would have an interest. So, off he went with Susie and other believers, leaving doubting Annie at home, painting.

When they reached the town where the mine was, they went to the town hall with their deeds to ask directions. Oh, yes, the clerk knew the place. The place where the mine used to be. The place where the mine had been abandoned and closed up a couple of years ago, the clerk said. All the mica was gone.

And there Louis stood, worthless deed in hand, ten thousand dollars in debt. His investors, back in Malden waited for good news and a return on their investment. When he arrived back in Massachusetts he immediately tried to contact the conniving couple. Of course, they had left town, with no forwarding address.

We can only imagine the conversation that took place between him and Annie. How could any marriage endure so many disasters, so many wrong turns? Financially, this was the final straw, because every penny must be paid back and it would all come from Annie's paintings. There would be no rest for her. And there would be no redemption for Louis. He had no more grand schemes in him. Poorer than ever now, they lost both homes to the bank, which allowed them to rent the one they lived in. Yet, they would be husband and wife with whatever was left of their relationship, courteous, kind and often showing warmth and affection still.

In a little birthday note around that time, that came with a coveted recording of Caruso, Louis wrote: *For my dearest Annie, to encourage her to sing, whose sweet voice is always an inspiration to me and to all others who are privileged to hear it. From her "chum" Louis*

chapter six

The peak of her career

In 1925, Annie and Louis, married for twenty years, were now in their late forties. During their mid-thirties they had witnessed World War I and the influenza pandemic that killed 43,000 in the USA and millions worldwide. Unbeknownst to them, the Great Depression would descend only four years hence. Their child was nearly eighteen and soon to graduate high school. Household finances were even more troubled due to the mica mine debts that Annie was determined to repay. But somehow, she must find college tuition for Irene. Perhaps because Louis was no longer available much of the time and Irene mostly beyond surveillance, Annie was able to spend more time in her studio. In any case this period was really the peak of her career.

She retained a New York agent and became one of the top competitors for freelance commercial art in New England. Although color photography was invented in the late 1800s, it was not until the late 1930s that it was used widely in mass publications. Also, early color photography did not have the delicacy and whimsy of paintings that the public had come to appreciate. So commercial artists were in great demand for attractive magazine covers, calendars, greeting cards, paper dolls, book illustrations and covers, advertisements, even billboards. In New England there were four women at the top of the market: Maude Tausey Fangel, Bessie Pease Gutmann, Jesse Willcox Smith and Annie Benson Müller.

All painted mainly babies and children, occasionally with a mother holding them. Companies that commissioned their work requested anything they thought would attract buyers. Little ones with a kitten or puppy, drinking a glass of milk, a boy with a frog, or, offering a flower to a shy little girl, reading a book, sleeping. One almost couldn't go wrong with an adorable child doing something cute. By one calendar company, Gram was asked to have babies doing adult things. She painted a diapered baby on a horse, another diapered toddler on a beach with a tangled fishing rod and one at a desk playing with an adding machine, with glasses sliding off his nose. Then there were seasonal requests. Gram painted three versions of the Madonna and Child for Christmas calendars, and cards for Easter with lilies. Her paintings were often lovely landscapes of gardens, small pools, flowering shrubs with a beautifully rendered bird and a small boy or girl looking enchanted.

But selling her work required continuing effort. She sent samples everywhere there were possibilities. Once she vied for the honor of painting the famous Dionne quintuplets for a paper doll company. Imagine the work of creating interesting wardrobes for five little girls plus their portraits. Then there were the paper dolls based on Princesses Elizabeth and Margaret, with their riding habits, and fancy dresses for royal occasions. She had to create the images only to be turned down each time. Time-consuming and very disappointing I am sure. But the public loved her work, and often sent her photos of their own babies in cute poses, hoping she would choose them as a model. She used some of Nell's babies in the early days, and Irene as well. But one child, whose mother was a professional photographer, was chosen for many pictures. His name was Jackie Duhamel. He seemed to fit the idea of the perfect baby of the twenties. Curly hair, sweet smile, expressive eyes, plump body. Think of Shirley Temple and you have the picture. Sadly there were no diversity initiatives in those days, so of course all the babies were Caucasian. But, they were Annie Benson Müller babies, quite different from her three competitors in their look and the scenes in which she set them. Many people saved the two magazines that bore most of her covers. One was *The Farmer's Wife*, a typical women's magazine with stories and articles on growing and cooking food. The other was *Modern Priscilla*, a needlework magazine full of patterns for delicate crochet, drawn work and embroidery. Even today one can find these magazines in antique shops that specialize in paper items. Mostly the companies that hired her kept the originals, but she managed to retrieve some. One of her great-granddaughters has collected many and set up a website on the Internet for people who still seek her prints and originals. She would be amazed and amused that forty years after her death people are bidding for her work on eBay.

For me the most interesting thing on her website is how people speak fondly of certain paintings that hung in their childhood homes. One person said she had had polio as a child and was confined to her bed for a whole year. One of Gram's paintings of a small girl in a beautiful summer garden, hung in her room. The writer said she pretended she could play with that girl in that garden and it helped her get through her ordeal.

Gram's deep love of children and the natural world are very evident in her painting. Her style was photographic realism done in watercolor paint and pencil. Every bird, bunny rabbit, squirrel, mouse, kitten or puppy showed how she delighted in the shape and beauty of the animal. Her flowers were equally expressive of the wonder she had for delicate petals and twining tendrils. And the details of every child's round head, shell-like ears, dimpled hands, and bright eyes, bear witness to her love of children. All these keen observations and more, speak of her reverence for beauty, her wonder in all creation, her joy in honoring that with her work. No matter how exhausted, troubled, or pressed to earn money, she never compromised her work to be less than her finest effort.

Once every few years she would take precious time to paint something for herself. The artist had things that needed to be said, rather than take dictation. So a small body of paintings were created that were never sold. One such piece is called 'Mother's Jewels,' a portrait of her first grandchild, my brother, at about one year old. He is sitting beside an open jewelry box, holding a necklace and looking up with a slight smile. Another is a much later painting of the Grecian bust that Louis gave her as a wedding present. She had wanted the challenge of painting white on white. So she set the alabaster bust against a white satin drape, with pearls and a white rose arranged in the foreground. Each white had a unique texture and tone and together made a fascinating study. At the time of this painting, I was about ten and loved to watch her work. She warned me not to disturb the table where she had set all these objects, as the background of white satin drapery was nearly complete and watercolor does not forgive as oils can. There was no way to correct or change the drapery if it was altered. I had no mischievous intention, yet my arm brushed against the table. The satin shifted. There was no putting back all the delicate folds to match what was already painted.

Most people in this situation would at least have expressed exasperation. And Gram would have been justified in raising her voice, perhaps really scolding me. But, that is not who she was. She simply put down her brush with a sigh. She said something about putting the painting away for now. I knew I had ruined it for her and felt terribly sorry, even crying. But she never said a word of blame ever.

About fifteen years later, I was to be married. There was a package in the mail from Gram, who was now seventy-four. Eagerly opening it, I found this precious painting, completed. In her letter she explained that she had taken it out and got the idea of repainting the background as black velvet. This allowed her to conceal the unfinished white satin drapery. All the elements of alabaster, pearls and flower now were in striking contrast to the velvet. She said in her letter that she believed that in the end the painting was even better than her original idea and gave me the credit. That incident illustrates perfectly how this remarkable woman dealt with every disappointment, every 'lesson,' as she would say. She was loath to place blame, to castigate others, rather seeking a way to understand them. My carelessness was attributed to my being a child. And she understood children with an uncanny grasp of psychology and developmental stages that was rare in one of her era. She had no space in her for self-pity or a grudge. How fortunate I was to have her example of courage and ingenuity as well as unconditional love.

Another painting of her own choice was inspired by a conversation she and I had when I was about eight. I had been practicing a piano piece called "Elegy," by Jules Massenet. I loved the piece because it had a very moving left-hand melody. But I was perplexed by the name. "Gram, what does Elegy mean?" I asked.

"Well, dear, it's things we might say about life and death. It's hard to explain. Thomas Gray wrote a poem called 'Elegy in a Country Churchyard.'" Then she proceeded to recite a few stanzas for me. I got the idea Elegy was something both beautiful and sad, and that was enough.

Toward the end of her painting life, she started a work called "Elegy." It shows the skull of a cow resting among dried leaves and delicate wild blossoms. Tucked close to the skull, she placed a bird's nest holding several tiny speckled eggs. On a small vine overhead, a song sparrow is perched and singing. In the distance, there is a suggestion of meadow and far-off hills. She was unable to finish the painting due to failing eyesight, but it is still lovely. And one sees her concept of life's cycle from birth to death, the mystery and beauty of creation portrayed in these simple elements.

Original paintings for commercial use were slowly replaced as improved color photography finally overtook the market.

However, Gram continued to receive occasional commissions and paint her own choices until the 1950s, when her eyesight was so dim that she could no longer distinguish the colors.

The only one of the four women who continued to do very well was Jesse Wilcox Smith, who had wisely diversified her subject matter enough to win contracts for children's book illustrations. Also Norman Rockwell, who was probably the best-known illustrator during her time. He was the only one to continue after color photography became the norm. He was best known for depicting American life on the covers of *Saturday Evening Post*, and his paintings of the Four Freedoms, for which he received a Presidential award. Gram was most admiring of his work always, not only for its artistic excellence, but for his humorous and respectful handling of scenes from ordinary people's lives.

Artworks by
ANNIE BENSON MÜLLER

A portrait of the artist taken during WWI. Facing financial ruin, Irene's adolescence, and the peak of her painting career.

The original icon for Bon Ami powder—its logo, "Hasn't scratched yet."

Hood's calendar, 1932, with author as model.

*Calendar
circa 1925.*

*Christmas Calendar,
1929. Irene, 20, with
son Daniel.*

Cover of Modern Priscilla magazine, 1922.

Modern Priscilla magazine, 1923.

A Christmas cover for Farmer's Wife magazine, 1923.

Portrait of author at 2 years

*Photo taken for
newspaper article
about the artist,
circa 1940.*

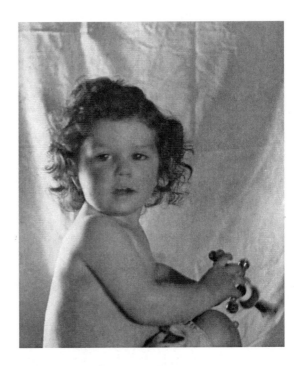

*Jackie Duhamel,
Annie's most
frequent model.*

chapter seven

Irene's choice

When Irene was a high school senior, she developed some problems with her feet and complained of significant pain. Annie had heard of a new Osteopathic physician in town that was reputedly very good. Louis seemed to accept this as a sort of Homeopathic medicine. So an appointment was made and mother and daughter went to see him. After careful examination he said that Irene's feet could be greatly helped with further treatment. On ensuing appointments Irene went without her mother.

Daniel E. Nyman, M.D., was twenty-nine and had been married for eight years to heiress Charlotte Pinkham. (Lydia Pinkham's Pink Pills for Pale People and some alcohol-laden Pinkham elixers claiming miraculous cures, were highly popular items in the '20s.) The couple had lots of money, no children, a nice home and shiny car. The doctor was slender, highly intelligent and a dedicated physician. He had a quick wit and winning smile.

Irene had become quite beautiful. She had been chosen as one of the models for a Boston photographer's convention where her exceptional hazel eyes, classic nose and delicate mouth were captured forever. At seventeen, she wore the short skirts, bobbed hair and gauzy, beaded fashions of a flapper. She had adopted a flippant stance, head thrown back, hands on hips, when she wanted distance, but also knew how to direct a disturbing gaze with those eyes. In her pictures she looks as if she was in her twenties.

Months passed and foot treatments continued. Included in treatment were invitations to accompany the doctor on house calls. He introduced her to his patients as his new nurse. Once, during a blizzard, he invited her to come watch him deliver a premature baby. She must have told her mother she was going for a walk in the snow. In any case her parents were not aware of her deception. But the doctor's wife was.

One afternoon, while Irene was at school, Charlotte Pinkham Nyman paid Annie a call. It must have been one of the most terrible days of Annie's life. I do not know everything that was said. But, Gram told me that Charlotte said, "Mrs. Müller, if your daughter does not stop seeing my husband I will kill her." She then opened her purse and drew out a small pearl-handled pistol. "And I know how to use this very well."

When Irene came in from school that day I am sure she lied and acted nonchalant, trying to make her mother's accusation seem foolish. Annie must have wanted to believe her and perhaps think that the doctor's wife was wrong. Anyway, in desperation, Annie decided to enroll Irene in a cooking school for the summer. That way she would perhaps have less time for mischief. Such a naïve and ineffective solution was useless for her totally out of control daughter. Poor Annie. Did she really think Irene would now trot to class all summer and resist the seduction of such an affair? Did she think Irene was still a virgin? That Dan was innocent?

This is every parent's nightmare of course. And Annie had no experience to prepare her. She had never been interested in flirtations as a young girl or even a young woman. Nor could she relate to deception. She valued truthfulness above all. And to have one's teen daughter in a clandestine relationship with a married, older man, would surely test the most sophisticated parent. Looking back, I don't think anyone could have successfully extracted Irene from the web she had now woven for herself. Nor did she want to be extracted. I sometimes wonder if it might have helped if Annie had shipped her off to Nell's house to help with the household tasks and child care. At least it would have created some distance and if not, Irene might have at least had a chance to get some preparation for what was ahead.

Nell, with her nine children and hardworking husband, was a loving aunt and very capable woman. Her take on life was quite different from Annie's and she might have been able to influence Irene to reconsider her future. Not only that, Irene might have realized how poorly prepared she was for homemaking and mothering. In any case, Annie did what she did. Cooking school it was. Meanwhile there was tuition to earn as well as the first year's expenses for Mills College for Young Ladies in California in the fall, as far away from the pearl-handled pistol as her mother could send her.

Irene pretended to go to Boston each day. The few times she actually attended classes she learned to make caramels, mints and spun sugar—not very useful items for feeding a family.

Later my mother told me that her first attempt to make bacon and eggs for my father had been really pathetic. She had seen a picture of fried eggs with the bacon strips nicely laid over the top. So she took a dry frying pan, broke eggs into it, and laid two pieces of raw bacon over them. Then she set this on the hot stove to cook. The result was scorched eggs with still-raw bacon hanging over the top and a ruined pan.

So, the summer after high school droned by with many opportunities for Dr. Nyman, now called Dan, and Irene to be together, in spite of Charlotte's threat; in spite of Annie's futile efforts. At the close of summer Irene got on the train to California. Annie handed her beloved daughter a dozen yellow roses. She must have hoped she had saved her from disaster and that college would help her settle down and get over this fascination with Dan. Irene would surely do well. She was bright and interested in many things. She was getting the opportunity her mother would have loved at that age. Everything had been pulled from the fire. All would be well, please God.

*Irene, 18, one of the
models chosen for
a photographers'
convention in Boston,
Massachusettes.*

*Daniel E. Nyman, M.D.,
31, when he met Irene.*

chapter eight

The party's over

Mills College was a very fine school then and still is. Its motto is, "One destination: Many paths." I doubt that Irene ever knew that, because she never even saw the campus. When she arrived in California, she did not go to Mills in Oakland, but instead took a room in a shabby boarding house in San Francisco. All she had with her was a small stipend from her mother for first semester and a trunk full of clothes and books.

She had good reason not to show up at the college. She was feeling very poorly. Everything she ate came right back up. She was three months pregnant with Dan's baby and losing weight rapidly. It was not just "morning sickness," but pernicious vomiting. To complete the disaster, one day she returned to her room to find the boarding house on fire. Everything she owned was lost. Most eighteen-year-olds would have the option to call their parents for disaster relief, but of course she wouldn't. Instead, she called Dan.

I would give anything to hear that call, because in my experience, my father was not a man who inconvenienced himself for others. I can imagine him telling her it was too bad, but not his problem. I take heart in the fact that in this instance he cared enough to take responsibility for her welfare and that of his baby.

His parents had been divided in their parenting methods. His mother had pampered him, her youngest and sickly child. His father thought severe beatings would cure his mischievous and delinquent nature. Neither method had helped the boy. By the time he was fourteen he had begun drinking alcohol to excess and impregnated the daughter of the police chief. To punish him, his father, who managed plantations for the United Fruit Company on the east coast, took him out of school and forced him to work in Florida as a picker until he suffered heat stroke. After he recovered at home, for his sixteenth birthday, his mother bought him a motorcycle. He drove it cross-country to Pike's Peak, which was a popular destination at that time. But he totaled the motorcycle. His mother was so grateful that he had survived, she bought him a car. Of course he would also smash that up while drinking and driving. On and on this cycle went until he eloped at twenty-one with the heiress, Charlotte Pinkham. I suspect his main motive was to secure a lifetime supply of money for his antics rather than being her kind and responsible husband.

When World War I erupted he found himself in the army. Perhaps he might have matured some had he even completed boot camp. But he was caught in the deadly influenza pandemic. His lungs were permanently damaged and he was given a medical discharge and life-long pension. He was twenty-two and had not completed any higher education. Somehow he managed to be accepted at the Chicago College of Osteopathic Medicine and graduated with an M.D. He honestly loved medicine and was very skilled in diagnostics. His patients adored him. He managed a very busy family practice for long periods and then would succumb to his alcohol addiction. He was a binge drinker, who might be incapacitated for a few months. Then he would recover enough to pick up his life again, until the next binge. Of course, Charlotte's money could tide them over, and he was still young enough to appear healthy.

These were the facts of his life when my mother had come to him with painful feet. Of course she knew that some people drank to excess and were drunkards. But she had no experience with normal social drinking at home. Only around the tables of her classmates' families had she seen wine drunk without comment. Annie and Louis were teetotalers, preaching strongly about the evils of alcohol. They considered drinking any amount to be the beginning of ruination. And drunkenness was seen as a disgraceful, willful, moral weakness. But Irene was coming of age during Prohibition where the speakeasy mocked the law. If Dan were to go on a binge while they were first involved, she, like all of his patients had probably been told that he was ill, or on a trip. So she had no way to assess this part of him during their early relationship. And even if she had realized that he drank to excess, I doubt that it would have changed her mind.

My mother's call from California was sufficiently appealing to cause my father to leave Charlotte and go straight to San Francisco to help her. They went to Mexico for a divorce, and drove up to Reno to get married. Neither action was considered legal in Massachusetts, yet they arrived home anyway, declaring that they were married. The pregnancy was still not going well.

Dan's parents refused to allow them into their home now. They were finished rescuing him. They were especially angry that he had left his wife so ignobly, and angry that he had involved a young girl in his disgraceful behavior. Dan's father and Annie formed a bond around their shared anguish about their children.

But Annie could not reject Irene now. She thought only of helping Irene get well enough to live through childbirth. Her doctor was concerned for Irene as well as the baby, for she now weighted less than 100 pounds at four months, with the baby due in April. In spite of everything she must have suffered from Irene's complete betrayal, Annie was so afraid that both Irene and the baby might not survive that she would not ever have turned them away. In fact, she and Louis begged Irene to come home until the baby was born. One would hope Irene would seek forgiveness and show gratitude. Instead, she played on their concern. She knew she had the upper hand and used it ruthlessly to make them include Dan in their offer. She announced that she would come home only if he could come with her. Actually he was homeless, but it must have been a bitter pill for them to agree to house him. They moved out of their bedroom to provide the best bed for the couple. All their anger toward Dan had to be swallowed daily. And rather than showing gratitude, he often complained if his meals did not please him. He actually demanded expensive cuts of meat, like lamb chops, which were rarely to be afforded in that house.

Louis tried to insert religious education on the scene, for he had a captive audience and they certainly needed something. He managed to read aloud some passages from *Science and Health* on occasion, I was told. The picture in my mind is poor earnest Grampa reading aloud to my young father, who would later ridicule and mimic him for my mother's amusement. And I can imagine her showing disdain openly.

Oh, what an unhappy situation for all! Yet, Annie's nursing care during the next five months did bring Irene back to health. On the 25th of April, 1928, just before she turned 20, she delivered a beautiful baby boy. They named him Daniel Currier Nyman. Currier was his paternal grandmother's maiden name. Annie fell in love with him. He was the son she never had.

Very soon, Dan and Irene moved to Arlington, a suburb north of Boston. Now they began married life without the extraneous drama of a romantic affair, challenged by a crying baby before they even knew each other as real partners. The tragic deficiencies of this young couple now became very clear. There was no one to fill in for all the skills of keeping house that Irene lacked. And she had little interest in child care. "Any fool can change diapers and wipe noses," she stated flippantly. So baby Daniel was frequently neglected and uncomfortable. Annie hired a housekeeper to help, but was still terribly concerned. Even worse, Dan had no patience with crying and would become enraged if his sleep was disturbed, even strapping the baby with his belt. There were his binges and many quarrels.

As baby Danny began to crawl and walk, getting into everything, as all babies do, neither parent understood. He was expected to behave like an adult. Irene would lock him out of the house and let him cry for hours as punishment. Annie offered to take the baby often 'so they could rest.' And they seemed glad to let him go. Exasperated by the demands of their child, they would bring him to Malden and literally dump him, soaking wet diapers and all. On one occasion they brought him over when he was very sick with a high fever, saying "Here! You take him. He's just impossible."

Danny was a very precocious, affectionate child who had easily discerned where he felt happy. So it was inevitable that he formed a bond with his grandmother that he had with neither of his parents. Soon, he would cry and beg to stay when his parents came to fetch him.

"You're just an old softie," Annie would be told, "you spoil him!"

All Gram was doing was treating Danny like the very young child he was. Giving him quality attention, such as reading to him, taking him for walks around the pond, teaching him to play simple games and showing interest when he tried to talk. As he grew he told her, "I love you, Grama. You always lean down to talk to me."

At home he received only Irene's casual, rather distant way of responding, and Dan's stiff and punishing stance. There were no welcoming laps or cuddling. He absorbed his parent's harsh criticisms deep in his heart, was anxious, strived to please without success. Gram related a time when he was still young enough to be in a highchair. He sat there with his bib on, tears running down his face. "Danny bad boy," he sobbed. "Danny bad boy." No amount of persuasion could change this sad understanding of himself. And such primal wounds do not heal easily. For Gram, the damage to her beloved grandson perpetrated by these two careless parents was nearly unbearable. She walked a tightrope lest they forbid her to see him, and made herself available always, trying to provide healing respite in the guise of simply 'taking him off their hands—toddlers can be so mischievous you know.' Any suggestions she offered about handling his behavior more intelligently or humanely were seen as interfering, or scoffed at, never heeded. And so it continued when their second child was born, just as Danny turned two.

She was a lovely little girl named Georgianna Beatrice, after Dan's mother and sister. Soon she was crawling and trying to play with Danny's blocks, which had been meticulously arranged in fragile towers. When his baby sister knocked them down, as all baby siblings do, Danny would go into a rage, for which he would receive enormous punishment with no redemption. "He thinks his toys are so damn precious," said Irene, failing to understand how desperately her children needed to be helped through all the days of growth as toddlers and siblings. Of course, all of us make mistakes as parents, but Dan and Irene were not even on the charts of normal.

And while my poor sister was barely 18 months old, I was born. At last my mother got to choose a name, Irene Dorothy. I was called by my middle name. She told me that Dorothy came from a memory she had of a birthday party she had attended when she was very young. It was the perfect party, she said, and the child's name was Dorothy. She associated the name with a happy time, and a happy child. A kind of sad yearning, it seems in retrospect.

By now, Danny was three and a half. Dan still binged and practiced medicine. Irene more or less managed three young children and probably had learned how to fry an egg or two. She still preferred to make caramels and spun sugar though. But the couple frequently farmed us out to willing caretakers. Gram usually took Danny, and Georgie and I went to the house of one of my father's childless patients, who loved caring for babies. These were not just afternoons, but sometimes month-long stays. Danny was fostered by a family who offered to adopt him. I don't know what my parents did while they were free of responsibility, but it was the thirties, and my father liked to drink.

Irene's concept of what children needed was radically opposed to Gram's. Irene had been vigilantly supervised and given every delight Gram could afford. All her early experiences had been carefully chosen to enrich, educate and nourish her, to give her a happy childhood. She was an only child who never had to share, or take care of a sibling.

Now as the mother of three children, her point of view was that children needed to figure things out for themselves, as she remembered doing. If a child wet the bed, it was a ploy for attention, because that's what she had done. If a child was hurt, they should not come running to her sniveling, but go back out and conquer what hurt them because she had not been taught to do so. If a child was hungry, they should go to the kitchen and find food. If a child wanted comfort in her arms, she would send them off to find something to do. In other words, don't expect her to pamper as her mother had done, because she had discovered that Gram's style of mothering had not prepared her for the real world. She wanted her three children to be tough and ready for anything. I can understand her logic but it needed radical tempering. It bordered on dangerous neglect.

One summer, the whole family took a cottage in New Meadows, at Bath, Maine. She wrote to her mother. "The kids, (3, 4, and 6) are having a great time. They play by the ocean all day, and at night fall asleep on the floor like puppies. They don't wake up even when we have an all-night party."

Our father thought we should learn to swim. So, one by one, he rowed us out into the icy, black ocean, tied a rope around our waist and tossed us over the side. "Swim!" he yelled. We splashed our arms and legs until he hauled us out. There was no teaching, or encouraging so it felt like angry punishment. We assumed we had failed to swim. And that was one of his better efforts as a father.

Irene arranged with a neighbor to have us all watch him butcher his pig. Like most children, we liked animals. We stood in the front of an open barn. The man hoisted a pig up by its feet. It screamed. He slit its throat. We saw lots of blood. When we came back to the cottage, terribly upset, Mama told us it was good to see things like this. She didn't want us to grow up ignorant like her, she said.

Had there been no children, Gram might have simply sighed and resigned herself to the fact that she and Irene would never meet on many levels. But her grandchildren, she felt, were suffering. And they were in real danger without sufficient supervision. Danny, in particular, was both emotionally and physically battered. We girls were more victims of neglect, sometimes wandering off into precarious places and being brought home by the police. Gram could not turn away under these conditions.

Irene, herself, had now become afraid of Dan if he had been drinking. There were incidents when he attempted to cook something while drunk and threw a frying pan full of hot oil across the kitchen at Irene, missing her, badly burning himself. Another time he tossed a lit cigarette into a wastebasket and fell asleep on the couch. My mother managed to douse it. Had we all been asleep, it might have been a tragic house fire. But the final blow to Irene's willingness to stay, came the night he took out his revolver. Dan had always loved guns, and liked to go to the police station for target practice at times. Being friendly with police was helpful at the times when his drinking might have become publicly visible.

On this night, my sister and I were playing on the floor. Our father was very drunk. He aimed the gun at us. Our mother dared not speak for fear of angering him. She was often the target of accusations about being unfaithful, or not making his dinner just so, or being a terrible wife in general. All that, as well as having all these annoying children that wouldn't be quiet when he slept and interfered with his life.

He pulled the trigger. The bullet made a groove inches between us on the wooden floor. He laughed and laughed. Then he passed out.

Although she still loved him, for the times he wasn't drunk and terrifying, for the times he and she still could laugh and enjoy each other, she knew she could not stay. So, while he slept, she gathered us up and called a friend who had a car to come get us. We took only what we wore and what we could carry that night. As we pulled out of the drive, my sister's memory is that of our father chasing behind the car, in his pajamas, brandishing a butcher knife.

Any grandparent witness to such events in the lives of their children and grandchildren can empathize with Annie here. And certainly Irene's action to leave was courageous and appropriate. She was demonstrating concern for our safety. But she had no means of support and few employable skills. The only jobs she had ever held were working in a doctor's office as a teen, modeling for painters and photographers and playing the piano and singing, for a short while, in a restaurant. Now, with three young children she was hardly free to take any job. Besides, it was 1934; The Great Depression. But she had been planning her getaway for a while, it seems.

chapter nine

Runaways

During the previous summer at Bath, Irene had swum out to a small island. To her surprise she met two young men camping there. They were Canadian and about 20 years old. One of them, Harry, was quite charming and they had kept in touch. On subsequent visits to the island, he and my mother carried on a flirtation. He moved to Boston, found work with a newspaper and had a car. He was the one she would call to rescue all of us on that decisive night.

Together they rented an apartment near Beacon Hill, Boston. My mother did not let our father know where we were, but left him a note. It said she did not blame him for his alcoholism, as it was a disease. (A very enlightened statement at that time.) But she said she was concerned for our safety. He was to send her some money for the children through Gram but could not be with us until he stopped drinking altogether.

In the 30s cohabitation of unmarried men and women was illegal. Yet Harry needed a place to stay, and added a sense of security for Irene. In exchange, he chipped in some of his pay and provided transportation. He was even-tempered and trustworthy and in love with her as well. So for a while, it worked. Danny was enrolled in first grade, Georgie in kindergarten and I in nursery school. Otherwise we played in the streets with the other urchins, unsupervised. Except for fear that our father would find us and air polluted with coal-dust that caused frequent bronchial infections, we were quite happy.

After that winter, we moved to South Boston. Our mother had decided the air would be better near the beach there. However, our new tenement was wretched. She had managed to get it rent-free because it was condemned. It was riddled with roaches and bedbugs, unsanitary and unsafe. But it was free if she would collect the rents for the landlady. So she did that, and Harry worked at the paper still, leaving us all to continue to run in the streets unsupervised. I believe that now even Annie was not told where we were, as Dan had recovered enough to begin looking for us. Amazingly, he had quit drinking entirely, but did not seek any help for his other problems of rage and violence. His goal was to punish Irene for leaving him. We knew something was happening because every now and then, a policeman or two would drop by and ask us a lot of questions.

"And where does Mommy sleep?" they would ask. "And who sleeps with her?"

Even at 3 and 4 years old my sister and I knew when to act dumb. We had been told not to tell cops anything. And we didn't. When we told our mother the police had been asking these questions she knew our father was closing in. Like a mother cat, she stashed us with a neighboring family. The following day, she was arrested for cohabitation and sent to the Charles St. jail. We would not see her again for nearly a year. I was given no explanation and left to imagine that perhaps I had been bad.

It wasn't difficult for the detectives to ferret out a family with extra children sleeping on the floor. So, after a few days, the police came with our father. I remember recognizing him by his fedora. I thought he looked like Dick Tracy. While our faux parents, being loyal to Mama, swore that we were theirs, our father pointed. "That one, that one and that one is mine," he said.

I was surprised that he knew who I was, as my child's mind had imagined he had forgotten all about us. While the neighbors continued to protest, the mother even weeping, we were carried down the stairs and out into an autumn night. Our father put my sister and me into the "rumble seat" of his Ford coupe and Danny sat up front with him.

During this fateful time, Dan had turned to Gram. They were both concerned for our welfare under Irene's laissez-faire child-rearing philosophy. The fact that she had 'run off' with Harry fueled their view that she was untrustworthy, immoral and unfit as a mother. Since Dan was no longer drinking and showed such determination to reclaim his children, Gram could empathize with him more than with her own daughter. I do not believe that anyone had actually asked my mother to explain why she left Dan, or why Harry was on the scene, or what her thinking had been. And had she explained, I doubt if anyone would have believed her. She was now the outcast, the persona non grata, the 'unfit mother.' Our father made sure that she would not even be allowed to visit us without his permission. And worst of all, her children would interpret these events with little encouragement to believe that their mother could have been a good person, in spite of her flaws.

It was decided that we would live with one of our father's patients. She was very poor and like many single woman during the Depression, 'took in children' to make ends meet. Dan certainly was not interested in taking us into his life. So that night, with no explanation, we were driven to a house and told we would be living with a Mrs. G. Suddenly, we were three strangers in an unfriendly house. Discipline was harsh for me. I was tied to a tree along with a skinny dog and my hands were smacked hard with the back of her hairbrush for anything that annoyed her. Even when I fell and got my hands full of splinters, she used the hairbrush.

Our father visited once a week to give her some money for our support. My sister dared to speak up.

"Mrs. G. is mean to us," she told him. He slapped her face. Bravely, she said she would run away if he made us stay there. Shortly, he moved us to the home of another patient in need of money. This was the woman who had cared for us a number of times when our parents had wanted respite. But she had never wanted full care of all three of us. She wanted only Georgie. Somehow Dan persuaded her to take Danny and me and there we were for the next four years.

We attended church and Sunday School every Sunday without fail. My sister remembers feeling loved and wanted. She developed a mother/daughter bond that lasted through her lifetime. But my brother was not given enough food, not allowed to leave the yard except for school, was stripped of his clothes and strapped with a belt when he talked back.

I was sent to stand in the corner for hours for wetting the bed, sucking my thumb or falling down and requiring a bandage. I was made to sleep in a crib and to sit with a bib in a high chair for not eating. Both Danny and I were malnourished. We heard little but scolding, damning rhetoric about how we would end up in reform school and God would punish us brats.

None of us were allowed to play anywhere outside of the back yard. We were locked in our bedrooms at 7 each night. Yet our father came weekly with the support money and approved of these methods of 'discipline.' He usually supplemented them with his own bad ideas.

In all fairness, he did make some efforts at times. He brought bags of candy and packages of gum once in a while. They were usually confiscated by our foster mother, however. He visited me when I had the measles and brought me Betty Boop paper dolls and a Popeye book. Remembering that his sister, Beatrice, was a graduate of the New England Conservatory, he paid for us to have piano lessons. And on the 4th of July he would bring Danny a bottle of Moxie and some rockets, while Georgie and I got sparklers. This was the extent of his ability to behave like a father. There were no hugs or conversation, and I have no memory of his ever taking us anywhere, like a day at the beach, a walk, or even for an ice-cream cone.

During those long unhappy years, we may have seen our mother three or four times. She and Harry were now married and had bought a house together. Her visits were strained. Somehow she expected that we understood that she was working to regain custody of us. It was typical of her to imagine that our thoughts were focused on the same issues that hers were. Actually, I found her difficult to relate to, for what I needed was reassurance that she loved me. A lap and a hug would have been good. But she would come and talk to me like a grown-up when I was barely four. I have a vivid memory of her leaning against the wall, smoking a cigarette and looking down at me.

"How do you figure it kid?" she said, blowing out the smoke.

I looked her up and down. She had on high heels, rouge and lipstick. She wore a short skirt. She smoked. All things I knew my conservative caretakers did not approve of. I wondered if she might pick me up. I wondered if she had brought me any candy. I wondered why we did not live with her any more, for in spite of her dangerous neglect, I had been much happier then. Then I had not wet my bed, I remembered liking food, I had not sucked my thumb or thought of myself as 'bad.' Now she asks me a riddle I cannot answer. I feel a total disconnect from this beautiful confusing woman I call Mama.

Enter: Gram. Although I had had contact with my grandmother sporadically since birth, my first real memories of her are when she visited us in this foster home. She arranged to take the train each Saturday afternoon, trudging up the hill with a full shopping bag in each hand. It seemed as though we suddenly had been found by our fairy godmother. Our guardians allowed us privacy in the front room. Gram would greet us all warmly with smiles and hugs. Then she would sit down and begin to take things out of the bags. Library books. A Mickey Mouse mug for me to drink my milk. Fresh green grapes. A scrapbook with an illustrated story about three children amazingly like us who had weekly adventures in foreign countries. I would always get to sit in her lap while she read aloud. Then she would give me extra attention as Danny and Georgie read their own books. She taught me to read from a first grade primer she had used when she was a teacher. And then she brought me my very own books too.

I realized that she loved us. Love meant that the other person actually listened to you and responded. It meant that you were seen and were important to them. This was a brand new experience for me. I sensed that my siblings cared for me, but then would conspire and tease me in mean and careless ways. Since there were no adults to intervene I had no concept of consistent, kind attention until Gram's visit. I decided to speak of the worries that filled my frequent nightmares.

"Do they put little girls in reform schools?" I whispered. Gram pulled back and said loud enough for everyone to hear, "Of course they don't put little girls in reform school! Who told you such terrible nonsense?"

The door to the room opened and our caretaker came in and ordered Gram to leave. They continued to talk in the next room.

"You come here and make trouble," she said. "They always behave very badly after you visit. You are not to come visit anymore." Gram tried to reason with her but was unable to get a word in. She left, walking down the hill to the train and turned back once to wave at us, clustered at the window. There were no more magical Saturdays now. Just more sadness and isolation.

Then one Sunday we were all in Sunday School and ready to be led upstairs to sit through an interminable, boring hour-long worship service as well. But, instead, we were herded back into one of the classrooms. There was some whispering, and then someone opened the small basement window, lifted me up and told me to squeeze through. As I emerged into the driveway outside I saw my grandmother standing there. She greeted me with a broad smile.

"There you are, darling," she said. "Come with Gram, and we shall sit together in church." I had no idea why I had been squeezed through the window, but was thrilled to see Gram. Evidently, she had decided that she could not be kept from coming to church, and the caretakers, having seen her there, thought they could sneak us out and take us home to thwart her. But they were the ones now thoroughly thwarted and reluctant to behave badly in public.

We all sat in the same pew, three of us jammed in around Gram. Our caretaker had a terrible scowl on, so I knew she was really angry and that made me anxious. But Gram acted as though everything was fine. She opened her bag and took out three Canada mints and passed them out to us. That increased the scowl of course. When I fidgeted, Gram gave me a small pocket mirror to amuse myself with. Later I was accused of flashing light into the Minister's eyes with it, although I had no idea one could do that with a mirror. I was made to stand in the corner all afternoon anyway.

But Gram's defiance and good humor had brought a ray of hope into my misery. The world was not all scowls and black umbrellas after all. There was this wonderful, happy thing called love. It was stronger than negativity. And love was synonymous with Gram. Her example taught me that even the smallest kindness contains great healing power.

chapter ten
Broken hearts

Now one of the most painful episodes in everyone's life was about to unfold. My grandparents had to make a decision that would forever alienate their only child.

Our parents had divorced and both had remarried. Mama had converted to Catholicism and she and Harry had bought a house in Revere, with a parochial school directly across the street. She filed suit for our custody. Dan immediately mounted his counter-suit. His financial resources allowed him to hire powerful lawyers. Irene had very little money and poor lawyers. She relied on the sympathy of the court and her beauty to carry the case. The stories told in court were eagerly picked up by the tabloid, *Boston Daily Record*. Doctor and beautiful model battle for custody of three tots. Our father made it clear that his goal was not to care for us himself, but to make sure she did not win. "I would put my children in an orphanage in Canada rather than see them with her," he stated. When asked by the judge why she had divorced Dan, Irene stated only that he was not himself when drinking. Hardly a strong illustration of the fearful events we had all suffered. Dan did not hesitate to describe her as an unfaithful wife, even though he too had strayed. But she did not retaliate. My eleven-year-old brother, Danny, was considered old enough to speak with the judge in his chambers. He stated that he would prefer to live with Gram rather than either parent.

All Georgie and I could do was slide up and down the glossy

marble floors in our Mary-Jane patent leather shoes, waiting to hear our fate. Had they asked our opinions they might have heard that I also wanted to live with my grandmother. The judge had ordered psychological examination for all three of us to assess our IQ and emotional health—quite an advanced step for the times. But all the tabloids reported was that "The Nyman children were found to be highly intelligent."

The trial lasted for nearly two weeks. The judge was now consulting with Gram and Grampa about the possibility of assuming guardianship, with our father retaining custody. They said that if a better solution could not be found they would be willing to do that.

Our grandparents were now nearly 60. They would be assuming full responsibility for three children, who now exhibited the results of years of emotional and physical trauma. We were angry, grief-laden, needy survivors; poorly socialized, rude and temperamental. To accept us would require testifying against their own daughter. Yet they were not willing to let her resume her brand of mothering.

I am grateful, for it is unlikely that Irene would have improved even given that last chance. But the custody trial was her undoing. A condemnation of her as daughter and mother, indeed, as a person, from which she would never fully recover. And her relationship with her mother, already deeply unhappy, would now be openly hostile for many years.

So, offering to take on three grandchildren was a courageous and heartbreaking decision for Annie. Her only child had become a woman she did not trust or respect and felt deeply alienated from. Yet she could not let the chaos continue for three children she deeply loved. And this painfully conflicted decision, this sacrifice, truly saved us.

When Irene heard her parents testify that she had been a dangerously neglectful mother, she realized that they were aligned with Dan and that she was battling against overwhelming odds. Now she decided to play her last card. I will never know whether she was advised by her lawyers to say untrue things that might sway Judge Bean's decision, or whether she really believed what she said. Both statements were shocking to the court and all concerned.

"Annie Müller is not my real mother," she said. "I am the illegitimate daughter of Louis Müller. Annie Müller could not have children, so she told everyone that I was hers, and raised me as her own."

Could that be true? Did that pregnant young woman that had come to the door two decades ago, saying she was carrying Louis child, have given her baby to them at birth? Proof was needed. With some difficulty, Annie managed to locate the mid-wife who had delivered her baby. She presented the court with a signed affidavit that Irene was indeed her birth-child.

Irene was now seen as a liar by the court. And whatever she said for the rest of her life would be seen as fabrication by her parents. However, she was still ready to make statements that might discredit her parents and give her some leverage in winning custody. She was desperate. She felt maligned, detested, alienated from her own children and parents. The wrongs that were done to her in her marriage to Dan were swept away, and the whole focus had become her carelessness as a parent. She had not beaten us, she was not a drunk or a prostitute. But she was a liar. And she had betrayed her parents' trust when she first became involved with Dan. The whole custody trial focused on her flaws, with little attention given to Dan's dangerous drinking, physical abuse, his stated unwillingness to care for his own children and the fact that he also had extramarital affairs. Money talked. Irene's case was doomed and she knew it. So, now she said, "My children must not live in that house."

"Why do you say that?" asked her lawyer. Looking directly at the judge, she answered.

"When I was a young child, my father molested me. If you allow my children to live with him, he will molest them too."

My grandfather gasped. His face turned red and then white. He nearly fainted. How could she say such a terrible thing? Everyone in the court was looking at him. Within weeks his hair would turn white. The papers never printed this accusation, but the shock to Louis would do permanent damage not only to him, but his relationship with my sister and me. He dared not be alone with us. He dared not touch us, or sit next to us. There would be a deeper cloud of sadness always around him now. On his deathbed he would say, "I wish Irene would come to me and say she didn't mean those horrible things she said about me in court."

But, Irene, as an old woman, would say, "It is good that these things can be talked about now. When they happened to me no one would have believed me." So she still believed that her father had molested her as an infant, though she had no recollection of it. She rationalized it by saying that that was why she was such a sickly baby.

As her daughter, and a psychologist who has worked with many pedophiles as well as abused people, I believe that my mother lied and came to believe her own lie. Firstly, my grandfather never exhibited any signs of pedophilia. He would kiss the top of my head as I practiced the piano, saying, "Sweet as a coconut." This was an affectionate, spontaneous gesture made as he passed through the room. He encouraged us to exercise and build up our muscles. Occasionally, I would show him my skinny little biceps and he would squeeze it, saying, "Just look at that!" or some other compliment. He never suggested we sit in his lap. He did not linger, or seek opportunities to be in our bedroom, or 'accidentally' enter the bathroom when we were undressed. He didn't do any of the things that would lure us into a compromising situation with him. He took me to Boston and showed me places of interest, like the waterfront and the fishermen, the Mother Church with its amazing glass bridge inside a globe. Made silly jokes. Brought home a special cage for my pet squirrel. He was just there, less involved than Gram, but always in the background as a kindly support. No, he could not have become this grandfather if he had been a man who molested his baby daughter. A pedophile would have manifested other behaviors living with two young girls for five years with every opportunity for relapse.

What my professional experience also taught me, is that people break under the kind of cruel stress that my mother suffered during her marriage, her single parenting and the custody trial. And I believe my mother had a psychotic break. In order to explain to herself why everyone had joined forces against her, she had to believe they could not be her real parents. In order to win her children back she had to turn the tables. She had to find something that would make them unsuitable. And she had been a sickly child. Her father had been concerned enough to try and feed her 'nature foods.' Her parents quarreled about her health care. And she sensed that he and her mother did not talk openly about their troubles. Annie, especially, was trying to hold on to her idealistic version of her marriage. Irene had no siblings to sort things out with. She was bright and imaginative. It was natural for her to make up her own stories about things. But, stating in public that her father had molested her was something that she could not easily erase. It had to become fact for her, forever.

Now the judge had a dilemma. But, it was very easy to favor our grandparents' calm dignity over Irene's desperate, dramatic statements. And he had my brother's solemn testimony that he did not want to live with either parent. So, it was decided that we would live with our grandparents. Our father would provide financial support. Our mother would be given only rare supervised visits.

She came out of the courtroom and reporters immediately surrounded her, asking what had been decided. She knelt on the floor with us posed around her for their cameras, her stylishly cocked hat mocking the genuine sadness in her beautiful face.

"Well, kids, we lost," she said.

She truly thought that we had been longing to reunite with her for the past four years, because that is what she longed for. And our grandparents' home on Vista Street was, for her, a place where she remembered only tension, restrictions and attitudes that she had not been able to reconcile since puberty. Certainly, her children would want to be with their mother out of loyalty. She had fought so hard for us against the vicious attacks of her enemies. She could not imagine our thinking, or our bond with the kind, consistently loving Gram and Gramp we longed to live with. These were people that she despised now, that she disowned. She didn't seem to understand how four years of negative rhetoric about her 'badness' had broken whatever frail connections we may have had before. In that distant time when she was barely ever present, when we three were basically on our own, climbing on the high roofs of tenements, running from neighboring child-gangs in the trashy alleys and streets, being dragged home to an empty flat by policemen trying to keep us safe. And her subsequent visits at the foster home that left us confused and distraught did more harm than good, for she never addressed our needs. She was, to us, like a strange adult who didn't know how to talk to or be with us comfortably. Our mother, who loved us dearly all our lives, who suffered beyond imagining by losing us, who barely managed to survive after that day, kneeling on the marble floor in her tragic pose.

I felt bad for her, but was so filled with new hope that I wanted to leap and shout for joy. But, I knew I mustn't, for it would hurt Mama's feelings. I must pretend I was sad. So I kept my face still and watched Mama for cues. The paper printed this tableau on the front page with headlines: MOTHER LOSES TOTS.

Our foster mother, strangely annoyed by the verdict, seemed

to have compassion for Irene. When we were getting ready to leave, she said, angrily, "Your grandmother will spoil you brats."

But nothing could dampen our relief. My sister jumped up and down crying "Yaysha!" a word she had coined to express joy. I held my face still lest I be punished for happiness.

Daniel, 11

Georgianna, 9

The author, 7

Grampa and Grama go to court, 1937

chapter eleven
All for love

Vista Street; a front porch tangled in forsythia, etched glass panels lighting the front entry, Gram with her arms outstretched to greet the weary pilgrims, Grampa a shadow just inside. Our father prods us up the steps and into the hall still inhabited by an antique goldfish our mother had as a childhood pet. He had seen her departure, the new baby grandson and now witnessed us peering into his round kingdom.

Papa starts unloading suitcases and boxes, Danny manfully following his lead. Grampa shows them where to put things in the bedrooms upstairs. Papa says goodbye and drives off. After the wars, abuse, nightmares, chaos, we wild things have somehow arrived, body and soul, at this haven.

We sit around a dining table, plates full of nourishing food served with Gram's good-natured generosity. No scolding or threatening here. My brother begins to feed his starved body with as many helpings as Gram can conjure up. She makes no comment when I taste only scant bits; half my milk, one bite of chicken. In foster care I had lost my healthy appetite and failed to grow normally. In her amazing wisdom, Gram handled this by saying nothing. She simply set the table and made mealtimes fun. Perhaps there would be a pretty cellophane straw by my milk glass. Nothing would be said when I blew bubbles before sipping. Having barely any experience with happy mealtimes, we often quarreled rudely at meals. Gram would interrupt us with an invitation to hear an episode from the travels of Odysseus, or one of the tales from Arabian Nights all told beautifully from memory. We would learn by heart, the complicated genealogy and wild shenanigans of the Greek Gods and Goddesses, and about Hiawatha, the Legend of Sleepy Hollow and King Arthur's Round Table.

Bedtimes are no longer confinement in locked rooms. Georgie and I are tucked into our mother's childhood bed. At the open windows curtains billow in the soft evening breezes. Slow headlights slide across the ceiling. Gram sits in the bedroom rocker with her autoharp and sings lullabies that Amanda sang to her 60 years ago in their little farmhouse in Maine. "The Modest Violet," "The Little Sandman," "Land of Nod." Danny and Grampa talk softly down in the kitchen over a second bowl of hot stew. All around us, security, peace, love, for the first time in our lives. And here is where Gram's incredible understanding and patience for this wounded child shone forth.

I sleep soundly and wet my bed; a nightly happening since the foster home. Gram simply sets up a cot, just for me, with no comment. She puts a stack of towels at the foot.

"See dear, if you wake up wet, just spread this over it and go back to sleep. That way you don't have to worry about disturbing Georgie. We'll take care of all that in the morning."

And this is a household with no washing machine, either. But still, there are no threats, no scolding, no endless hours in the corner, no shaming. She simply practices positive reinforcement theory decades before it had been published in journals.

Another regressive behavior that I had developed in the foster home was sucking my thumb. My father and the foster mother spent many sessions contriving punishments for this evil. There was pepper sauce painted on my thumb, mitts sewed to the arms of my pajamas and ridicule. I was made to sleep in a crib and sit in highchair with a bib on for 'acting like a baby.' Yet in Gram's care I have no memory of ever sucking my thumb. I no longer needed that reassurance. The anorexia and bed-wetting took many years to disappear though, even in the presence of all that love.

When we started school we were weighed and measured routinely. The school required me to have an X-ray to rule out tuberculosis due to my low height and weight. Gram tried to get me to nap as I was extremely active. Perhaps I would have been diagnosed as hyperactive in today's world. But my long experience of seeing bed as a punishment made it impossible to nap. Again she found a way.

Early after my arrival, I was watching her paint a picture of a baby in its crib drinking milk from a bottle. I had a keen yearning to do the same. Feeling a bit ashamed, I shyly asked Gram if I could just try the baby's bottle. She let me put some water in it and drink. Then she suggested that milk would taste better. She went on to say that if I climbed into my sister's doll carriage, placed under the shade of the Linden tree in the yard, she would let me have a whole bottle of creamy, cold milk. Shortly, I was happily regressed, curled up in the carriage with my bottle and asleep for two hours. She had accomplished her goal of getting me to take more nourishment and nap in this ingenious way. Nobody shamed me for 'acting like a baby.' And after a few similar episodes I no longer yearned for the bottle or the carriage. Any modern day child psychologist would consider her a brilliant therapist. And, to this day, I prefer napping in an outdoor hammock to going up to bed. I know, today, that her therapeutic handling of my regressed behavior was crucial to my ability to begin to thrive again.

Because the wars of our parents would never cease, the fallout would seep even into this sanctuary, where we were to stay for only five years. So Gram's deep understanding and patient methods were crucial elements in our ability to begin to heal and grow. There is no question in my mind, that had she not intervened, our lives could not have been as successful as they have been.

There were many things we had not yet learned. We had never

eaten a meal in public, for instance. Aside from church attendance we did not know the simplest social courtesies. We knew only the strange extremes of managing ourselves in the slum streets within urchin groups, or the stultifying isolation of one backyard with no playmates. Our sibling bond was an attempt to replace parents, with authority on Danny's shoulders, interpretation on Georgie's and compliance on mine. Occasionally, alliances would shift and Georgie and I would conspire against Danny, or Danny and Georgie would plot complicated teasing sessions for me. But, basically we were an inseparable trio when threatened. Danny needed freedom to socialize with other boys, and to relinquish anxious responsibility for our safety. Georgie needed to be encouraged to develop her exceptional talent in both art and music, and surrender her role as judge and jury. After all, the adults she had known had needed someone to hold them accountable. I needed to feel seen and heard; to experience, for the first time a sense of my own person. And we all needed to grieve for our losses. There was never to be a home with a Mama and Papa where we were the beloved children.

Some months after we had settled in, Gram decided to give us a special treat. Downtown in Malden was an elegant ice cream parlor called "The Palace of Sweets." Gram had taken Irene there many times as a child and the owner was fond of her. She wanted to introduce Irene's children to him. So we put on nice clothes and walked to the Palace.

Inside were glass cases filled with hand-made chocolates. The whole place glittered with polished brass. The owner greeted us warmly. Gram ordered four hot fudge sundaes and we sat in a little booth to wait.

The waitress brought us a vision of whipped cream topped with a cherry in silver cups. We all began to enjoy our treats when Danny noticed that Georgie's whipped cream mound was higher than his. This annoyed him immensely. You have to remember that in the foster home he had been deprived of food and Georgie had always been favored. To rectify this injustice, he reached across the table and scooped up some of her cream for himself. She retaliated by reaching over and scooping out some of his. It was a fencing match with spoons. They argued loudly, trying to justify themselves and enlist Gram's support. From experience, I sensed that they might turn on my sundae next, so grabbed my cup and slid under the table gobbling as fast as I could. Mama's survival training had prepared me nicely for such events.

Gram put down her spoon and stood up. In a firm, flat voice we had never heard before, she said, "Come along children, we are leaving right now!" She walked out the door without looking back. We hustled after her, our uneaten treats left sadly melting in their silver cups. Danny ran ahead and caught up with Gram. He tried to joke with her, knowing how fond she was of him. Surely she would smile down at him. But no, Gram looked straight ahead and ignored him. He began pleading, saying he was sorry. She remained silent all the way home. Georgie and I walked behind them, aware that his efforts were not working. I was afraid, for I had never seen Gram angry and silent. Yet, something in me believed that everything would be all right in a while. It was an awakening I shall never forget. One does not get to stay in paradise when one behaves badly, but there is forgiveness.

After we arrived home, Gram told us firmly to go up to our bedrooms and be quiet. We did not argue. After an hour or so, she trudged up the stairs for the first of many long 'talks' with us.

This was how she disciplined. She spoke about respect, appreciation, kindness and self-control. Her talks were sprinkled with quotes from Emerson, Shakespeare, the Bible, Ben Franklin, ideas about human relationships and character. I, for one came to dread these philosophical sessions more than a spanking, which was so much quicker. To alleviate my boredom, I would hang by my knees from the foot of my bed, swinging slowly and watching her mouth open and close. However, as an adult, I realized that the values she shared were those that have sustained me forever, in spite of my insolent posture. And when Gram was done, she would reach out her arms, saying, "Come here, dear." And I would climb gratefully in her lap, bury my face in her neck and whisper, "I'm sorry Gram." She would hug me a while. Then we would go downstairs and have a cookie, or some grapes. All was forgiven and the incident was never mentioned again. And so it was on the day of the fateful sundaes. We were forgiven. But we were not invited to have such a treat again for many, many months.

Even as we became more secure in Gram's care, we still tried her in many ways. At the table Danny might echo our father's rage. "If you don't eat your food I'll come over there and shove it down your throat," he would shout at me. "You shut up!" I would shout back hurling my fork across the table at him. That behavior would cost me banishment to the bedroom and a long lecture about self-control, while Danny was lectured about bossiness. Our vocabulary was laced with the angry words of our previous caretakers. "You brat!" "I hate you!" "Shut up!" "I'll slap you!" Gram soon listed them as forbidden in her house. When she was exhausted she sometimes would look to the heavens and say, "Give me strength." And once, my sister and I mocked her. We looked up to the heavens, put on martyrs' faces and said in sugary voices, "Oh, give me strength." Gram simply looked at us and we ran outside, giggling loudly. On rare occasions, Gram abandoned patient reasoning, such as when Georgie and I would have a pinching fight, very loudly chasing each other through the house and slamming doors. Gram would go outside and cut a switch from the lilac bush, order us up to our room and switch our legs as we ran up the stairs. Georgie once screamed so loudly that Gram tied a dishtowel around her mouth. Not tight enough to hurt her though. When we were grown, Georgie told me she screamed because she enjoyed the sound of her own voice. And she did go on to sing professionally as an adult with truly lovely voice.

But, I can't blame Gram one ounce for those mild little switches. We certainly were very rude, uncivilized brats, (yes, there is no other word to describe us properly) to try the patience of such a dear woman as she. Her rare switches never hurt my soul the way rejection and ridicule had done. And she still truly believed that love could conquer all. The blackboard in the kitchen was even inscribed with the Biblical quote, "Love never faileth."

Although Danny and Georgie managed well in school, I did not. I flicked ink-soaked wads of paper at my classmates and chewed gum after repeated warnings. I brawled on the sidewalk with rude boys. Gram knew the principal from my mother's school days and they collaborated. I was chosen to draw a poster in the principal's office, for an hour each day. Georgie was often asked to draw posters because she showed artistic talent. So I was quite pleased to be asked to draw some too and behaved quite well for a while after that assignment. But I needed repeated reinforcement and soon was behaving badly again. Gram decided, with my teacher, to have me carry a conduct card to be marked daily. When I kept 'forgetting' to bring the card home she tied a ribbon on it and made me wear it around my neck. "Here, dear, this will help you not to forget." I was a little shamed by this, but the shame came from a developing conscience rather than anything she said. Needless to say, my behavior quickly became satisfactory again and I was praised. Again, it was Gram's diligence and abiding love for me that turned me toward more positive choices.

At home, I needed to be outdoors nearly all the time. Rather than restrict me Gram made me a pair of overalls out of some of Danny's outgrown corduroy pants. In 1938 girls simply did not wear pants, but Gram knew that my need to be active was restricted by dresses. She then came out in the yard and carefully instructed me how to climb my beloved Linden tree.

"Always make sure you have a solid handhold before you reach for the next branch. Now place your foot squarely on a good-sized one before you move up. There, Dot. That's it."

She walked up onto the terrace with me and showed me how to scale the boulders there safely as well. I never fell from rocks or the tree, which I often climbed to the very top, swaying in what I called my 'crow's nest" pretending I was a pirate, with the nearby pond, my ocean. On a rainy day, she allowed me to use the dining room chairs as 'islands,' the rocking chair as my ship. She made me an eye-patch and a Jolly Roger flag for the rocking chair. She would close the doors and let me leap from chair to chair noisily yelling out my version of pirate language. "Ahoy, ye lubbers! Avast me heartys!"

She fashioned a whip for me with a bamboo handle. I learned to crack it nicely and whip any tree in the yard; a healthy outlet for all the years of abuse behind me. I was allowed a cap gun and holster that I wore every day after school. She bought me roller skates that I nearly lived on in the summer. In the winter my ice skates would go on at breakfast and come off at supper. And there was the Saturday walk downtown to the library. I would push one of the dining room chairs right over the warm register and read voraciously all afternoon. She even allowed comic books, but not happily. Once, when I failed to put my Captain Marvel comic down when called to lunch, she slid it from my hand and dropped it into the stove without a word. She abhorred the mesmerizing effect they had on me, which was similar to the effect of video games on today's children. One Christmas I received my heart's desire; an Indian brave's outfit complete with bow and arrow. She gave in to my begging and pretended she was a bear and let me 'shoot' her with my rubber tipped arrow, drag her across the floor and prepare a pretend fire to cook her. Another Christmas I received a violin, which I had longed for. She and Grampa went without many things to save the money for that, and they endured my squawking practice sessions for the next four years. She made sure Georgie and I learned every needle art there was. We knitted, crocheted, sewed some simple garments and embroidered under her tutelage. We had a French club and learned vocabulary from hand-painted cards and read the tales of Madame Souris. On a rainy day she might cook molasses for a taffy pull. Hot summer days, she would turn on the hose and let us run under the sprinkler in the back yard. Each year we visited the Boston Museum of Fine Arts, where Gram introduced us to her favorite exhibits, until we could independently explore the exhibits we most enjoyed. The Peabody Museum with its dioramas and famous glass flowers were favorites. Although summer heat bothered Gram a lot, she took us on the ferry to Nantasket beach annually, for swimming and fun on the gentle amusements there. A short hike from Vista Street allowed wonderful nature walks in the woods and a picnic. She would always pack hard-boiled eggs with little portraits of us drawn on each one. I especially remember her holding her bird-glasses steady so I could see an Indigo Bunting. Another time we stopped by a farm where we bought goat's milk and were allowed to take home a tiny kitten, who we named 'Figaro.' Later, at the pet store, we each chose a different colored guinea pig and had the fun of breeding them to observe hereditary color patterns. We eventually had twenty-four multicolored squeakers. In short, she taught us how to find beauty and cultural enrichment everywhere even with very little money. Often, after one of our excursions, we would have supper at a local fish market, where one could buy a whole bucket of steamed clams for $1. Enough for all of us to enjoy. And by this time, we had learned our manners, believe me.

It is hard to imagine how she spent so much time with us and still kept up with her painting commissions. There was always a baby in progress on her easel and when it was shipped off, we waited for the check, because we might have only a few shovels of coal left. She would come home from the bank with several hundred-dollar bills and let us examine them before tucking them away. She would take a small amount to celebrate, with ice-cream cones all around, or a more tender cut of meat. Often, when money had run out, we would heat only the kitchen with old newspapers. Our breakfast might be stale bread spread with a little butter, sugar and cinnamon, and weak tea. But we never felt poor, because Gram maintained her good humor and generous loving attitude always. A luxury like running hot water was unknown to us at Vista St.. Georgie and I would share a bath of about one inch of warm water lugged upstairs in teakettles by Gram. We thought it was wonderful to splash each other and play with the soap bubbles until Gram would pick up the cold spray and chase us around the tub to get us clean. Then, all powdered and tucked in, we would listen to the beautiful music box until we fell asleep. And she would be downstairs doing supper dishes, and finally at her easel until late at night, painting uninterrupted. She must have been very tired when morning rolled around and we three needed breakfast and clean clothes for school. But every day, she was there, cheerful and loving anyway. When my sister and I would burst through the door after school, she would call out from her studio, "Hello my darling girliques!"

I write this just to illustrate how happy those years were for us in spite of our beginnings. She civilized us and gave us ethical principles for life. In every way, she demonstrated unconditional love. She showed good humor and courage in very trying financial uncertainty, and gave us the lifelong gift of joy in simple things.

But there were some aspects of parenting that Gram missed. And, they were the same items that she failed to teach our mother.

We were never asked to help her by making our beds, washing dishes or sweeping a floor. By the end of five years, I was nearly 13, Georgie 14, and Danny 16. Danny had had several jobs that he initiated himself. He had wheedled a bike out of our father and got a paper route. He walked into a music store and asked to try out a new electric organ there. He played so well that they hired him to demonstrate the organ to customers. He got a job playing marches for the exercise class at a local gym. And with his money, he would take me on the front of his bike to a discount warehouse he knew, and together, we would pick out flowered cotton housedresses and aprons for Gram when hers got shabby. He paid for my sister and me to take swimming lessons at the YWCA in Boston. He bought us a beautiful anthology of piano music to augment our lesson books. But he didn't do household or yard chores. When we offered to help with laundry, cooking, or mowing the lawn, Gram would gently discourage us. She even braided my hair every morning for me before school. So, I was unready to care for myself at all. And that would lead to considerable unhappiness when I left her home. I think she felt that we had not had enough care and was trying to make it up to us. Also, housekeeping was low on her list of things to do. She would rather go on a hike or to a museum. So spending time teaching us to wash a floor or make a simple meal didn't appeal to her. It was a crucial gap in her understanding of what we needed, and what my mother had needed.

It is actually very difficult for me to point this out as a failing, as I am so grateful to her for all she did do, and can hardly bear to criticize her. But, examining her life, as she did, always asking herself, "Where did I go wrong?," this particular lack seems to be a culprit in each instance. Her early letter, where she expressed her hope for an ideal marriage and envisioned the happiness of others dependent on her selfless love, is the key. Had anyone of wisdom been able to suggest that she consider shared responsibility with Louis and teach her child practical skills for independent living, things might have gone better.

chapter twelve

A mother lost

The other aspect of our five-year reprieve that was not idyllic, were those times when Mama surfaced. She could visit only by permission and facing her parents after the custody trial could not be made pleasant. Everyone would be civil, but extremely uncomfortable. The first encounter came when Georgie was 9. She had appendicitis. Grampa argued that he would heal her with Christian Science treatments. Papa came flying to Vista Street to tell him firmly that Georgie would be going to the hospital for surgery immediately. Because she was extremely distressed by this replay of her childhood, Mama was allowed to come see Georgie before surgery.

Mama now called her mother 'Madam.' Even so, Gram kindly let her come to our bedroom alone. As usual her behavior was not anything that one might expect. We hadn't seen her since the trial, well over a year. Yet she entered the sickroom like some whirlwind. Instead of hugs and quiet greetings, she was boisterous.

First she proposed that we play charades. We didn't know what she meant, so she demonstrated the word, 'Madagascar.' I leave it to you to envision her antics acting out this word as Georgie, with the pain of appendicitis in her belly, watched from her bed, and I wondered what the hell Mama was doing and why. It was such a bizarre encounter. Finally, she finished. I think she kissed Georgie and said something cheerful to her before leaving. But she ignored me completely. I remember feeling that my ignorance about charades had disappointed her.

Without our knowledge, Mama had decided to find a way to discredit her parents and mount a further effort for custody. To do this, she decided to enlist the help of Mrs. O'Neil, who lived across the street from Gram. Mama had converted to Catholicism in order to marry Harry and now used that card to gain Mrs. O'Neil's trust. The O'Neils were the only Catholics on Vista Street, and were polite neighbors, though not close friends of Gram and Grampa even though their daughter and Irene had been childhood playmates. Mama repeated her claim to the O'Neils, that Gram had adopted her and that Grampa had abused her as a small child. She also said that she had been starved at times when Gram forgot to feed her. Mrs. O'Neil, having no sense of loyalty to Annie and Louis, swallowed Mama's horrific accounts whole. She agreed to help her by watching us closely and reporting anything she could to the authorities.

Her first act in Mama's behalf was to feed us. One day as we walked by her house coming home from school, we heard, "Psssst! Girls!" We stopped and went closer. She did not invite us in.

"Are you girls hungry?" she asked. Well, we were a little hungry after school, so we said yes.

"I just cooked some corn on the cob," she said, disappearing into her kitchen. She came out and handed each of us a hot, buttery ear of corn. "Eat it right here, girls, but don't tell your grandmother. You can always stop by here if you're hungry," she said, looking very sad. We wondered why she thought we wouldn't just ask Gram for something to eat. But, before we could ask, she shut the door. We stood there and devoured the delicious treat, then ran across the street, empty cobs in hand. "Gram! Guess what? Mrs. O'Neil gave us corn on the cob," we said. After a few calm questions, Gram walked over to the O'Neils' house. She thanked her neighbor, who was obviously flustered. It took only a few minutes for Gram to figure out that Mrs. O'Neil was Mama's pawn in a wicked game of chess.

Gram leveled with us. "Mama has told Mrs. O'Neil that I am not feeding you enough. Mrs. O'Neil doesn't realize that Irene is lying to her. You have my permission to stop by there any time if you like her treats." So, with that in mind, we accepted some great treats, like hot, fresh donuts, before Mrs. O'Neil made her next move to 'protect' us.

That was to call the Board of Health and tell them Gram kept pigs in the cellar. A courteous official came to inspect.

"Mrs. Müller, we have a report that you are keeping pigs in your cellar, which is against the law. May I come in?" he said. Gram knew immediately that this was Mama's spy across the street, relaying misinformation. "Of course we do not have pigs in the cellar. My grandchildren have only some pet guinea pigs. Please come see for yourself." On the way to the cellar she told him briefly about Mama's current attempts to regain custody by making her look bad. The agent laughed when he saw the pens with our Rusty, Inky, Vanilla and their progeny. "Oh dear. This is too bad," he said. "But, your neighbor is determined to make trouble. Perhaps if you could bring these cages outdoors we could tell her the problem has been rectified," he said.

So, while we were in school, Gram carried all the cages outside and set them up on the front porch. It was warm weather, and she felt she and Grampa would have time to procure better housing for our precious pets before the cold.

But for now, Mrs. O'Neil would have nothing to rant about.

Georgie and I still walked home for our lunch and this day came up on the porch, surprised to see the cages there.

But, when we looked in at our pets, every single one of them was dead, bloody and mangled. We ran to Gram, sobbing. Nearly in tears herself, she told us that two roaming dogs had come on the porch and killed them. She had not had time to conceal the carnage before we came home. She comforted us as best she could, feeling terrible that she had not been able to prevent this totally avoidable traumatic loss for us. Needless to say, Mrs. O'Neil was our enemy now and Mama was colored with the same dark brush.

We never knew if our mother felt sorry about our pets. But, she was still agitating Mrs. O'Neil to cause even more trouble. Her next ploy was to cause trouble between Gram and other neighbors next door. They had rented a room to a single gentleman who had a wire-haired Terrier, Rowdy. One day the man and his dog stopped by to chat with Gram and Danny out front. Danny played with the dog in a rather rough way, getting him quite riled up, until told to stop. After Danny had left, I came out, not knowing that Rowdy was not wanting any more children around right then. I approached him and he lunged at me and bit deeply into my thigh. His owner and Gram were horrified, and I was hustled into the house for first-aid. Gram called my father to report the incident, and he came right over to try out a new cauterizing machine on my wound. I was fascinated by all medical things and loved attention from Papa, so the incident was not very traumatic to me. For about six months I crossed the street when I saw a dog, but was soon patting every one I came to again.

Then, our neighbors called Gram with terrible news. Rowdy had been poisoned and died. His owner was devastated. And Mrs. O'Neil started a rumor that Gram had poisoned him for biting me. The neighbor, Mrs. Rounds, wanted Gram to know that she didn't believe this for a minute, but thought she should tell her what had been said. This lie about my grandmother made me very angry. So I decided to seek revenge against Mrs. O'Neil for all the pain she was causing us. One day, Mrs. Round's granddaughter and I were playing when I spotted Mrs. O'Neil plodding up the hill, breathing heavily, for she was a large woman. Quickly, I persuaded the other child to hide with me in Gram's forsythia bushes. "Let's say, 'Here comes Fatty O'Neil,'" I said. So, as she approached, we called out our rude greeting two or three times, thinking she couldn't possibly guess who was saying it. My heart was beating fast with excitement and I thought this was a very clever way to settle the score. I had reverted to my slum urchin skills in this instance.

However, when she was nearly abreast of the bushes, she stopped and glared in our direction. "I can see you," she said in a nasty way. My heart sank. Then she went into her house and called Gram to report our insult. Gram's reaction was muted. Although I knew that she certainly did not approve of what I had done, she did not show the shock or sternness I expected. Her chief concern was that I had involved Mrs. Rounds' granddaughter and that I should apologize. So there were some calls between them. And Mrs. Rounds, bless her heart, said, "Oh, Mrs. Müller. After all the trouble that woman has caused you and the children, I wouldn't make that poor child apologize for what she did." And aside from a small lecture on kindness, I was not punished. Even so, I learned that my behavior was wrong in that instance because it had caused Gram grief.

Meanwhile, Irene's thinking was that she was merely fighting to get us back. Who could criticize her tactics in such a war? She had been crushed. She would develop elaborate explanations.

One of these involved money that Dan's parents, now dead, had left him. There was an ample trust fund that he could draw upon for 'dire emergencies.' He had managed to convince the trustees that his legal battles qualified. Then there was a trust fund left by his father specifically for our education. It would have paid for all three of us to attend the finest colleges in the country. Unfortunately, our father had access to this fund. Rather than support us with his ample earnings, he used our educational funds to pay for our board wherever he chose to park us. Consequently, at college time, there was no money left for our education. This is just another example of the unscrupulous man against whom Irene was fighting. She had received no money from him after their divorce, even for our support. So, her assessment was quite accurate that he was ruthless and powerful. Now, she felt, since disowning her parents, that they were also ruthless. And she imagined their motives for keeping us included getting access to Dan's money. After all, money had always been terribly scarce at Vista St. and Louis had a reputation for striving to strike it rich. If you couple these facts with my mother's terrible loss, her sense of alienation and isolation from all who once had claimed to love her, it is not hard to see how she might fabricate explanations that avoided deeper truths. Those truths would have revealed her own failings. And she was not able to bear them. How could any mother admit that she put her own children in jeopardy? Especially, since she sincerely had felt she was saving us.

But, of course, at 8 or 9 I could not begin to understand the reasons behind Mama's behavior. It would be many years before she and I had a relationship of mutual respect. For now, she was a very disturbing intrusion. Like a hornet's nest erupting in the middle of a picnic. And even worse, the negative comments I heard constantly about her from everyone, including my siblings, seeped into my sense of self. If my mother was so bad, I felt I must be bad too. It was not a logical thought, yet children often come to these conclusions when adults around them are quarreling.

So, trying to raise us was not a simple matter. Our Vista St. sanctuary was constantly besieged; fraught with one disagreeable event after another. Mama's next ploy was to stake out Vista Street, waiting for Gram to leave the house. Gram did all her grocery shopping on foot, so she went out frequently so as not to have bags too heavy to carry. She sometimes took the train to Boston to meet with someone who was commissioning her work and might be gone for nearly the whole day. But these were rare occasions and Grampa or Aunt Susie were usually home for us.

But one day, everyone was gone. Gram was concerned about our being alone. She told Danny he could go to his job, but asked us to stay at home, which we did. Around noon some strange man in a black car parked in the driveway. Mama stepped out of the car and came right into the house. She did not greet us, but went upstairs to our grandparents' bedroom. She said, "You kids sit on the stairs and be my look-out. I need to get something." Even though we knew she was not supposed to be in the house, we obediently sat on the stairs. We heard her opening and shutting drawers in the bedroom as we watched the front door. Finally, she came down, her arms full of papers. "Now don't say anything about my being here when Grama comes home." Out she went, driving away in the black car with the strange man.

When Gram came home, we could hardly wait to tell her what happened. We had been scared. But, worse, we had felt as though we betrayed her by letting Mama enter the house. Yet we were too young to stand up to her. All of this came tumbling out. Gram went upstairs and we heard her gasp as she saw her personal things strewn on the floor.

What Mama had been looking for was letters she had written to Gram. She remembered Gram reading her letter aloud to the judge in court, about how we slept like puppies on the floor during house parties that summer in Bath, as an example of her careless parenting style.

So, now Gram knew that she must be preparing for another trial. She did not scold us for letting Mama in. She simply decided that she would never put us in such a situation again. For what was stopping Mama from kidnapping us? Somehow, someone persuaded Mama never to come to Vista St. again without permission. It was probably one of my father's lawyers.

Several days later, Georgie and I came out of school. There, parked in front, was the black car with the strange man in front. Mama called to us. "Come on. We're going to get ice cream." The whole thing felt wrong, yet we got in the car. The man started to drive slowly in the wrong direction. Mama spoke from the front seat without looking back at us.

"So! You're a couple of squealers? You told Gram that I was

at the house? Squealers. What kind of kids would squeal on their own mother?"

I began to worry how far away we were going, when the man pulled over and parked the car.

"Now, get out of my sight, you squealers," said Mama. We climbed out quickly and they drove away. I thought sadly about the promised ice cream, but knew better than to mention it. I was just grateful to be free. Georgie and I were both subdued as we walked home to Gram. We told her about our encounter. Again, I think a restraining order of some sort must have been issued, for Mama never showed up like that again.

After a time of calm, Papa and Gram negotiated with her to drop pursuit of custody and settle for more frequent visits. We were about 12 and 14 now and considered old enough to take public transportation to Revere, where she lived. It was a city by the ocean, with a mini-Coney Island amusement strip. And even though, on our own, we had never asked to visit her, we were somewhat curious to see her environs, and also liked the feeling that finally it could be our choice to see, or not to see, our mother.

Since WWII had erupted, Harry had been in the Army leaving Mama alone in their large house, within walking distance of the beach. She rented rooms to transients for income, and possibly to feel less vulnerable and lonely. Most of her roomers were servicemen and their 'wives' awaiting orders to go overseas within a few days. At first we visited only for the day. Mama would give us each a whole dollar to go down the hill and enjoy the amusements. Not much of a visit. As time went on, with no untoward incidents, we were allowed to spend one night, as long as Danny was with us.

Although Mama always seemed happy to see us, she also seemed unable to really spend time with us. After all, we were essentially strangers with a checkered history. She would invite one of her neighbor's children to spend the night too, and invariably it was a child several years younger than I, as if she had forgotten my age. Then she would spend most of the time telling me all about the other child. I always felt she liked the other child better and withdrew emotionally.

This is Twinny," Mama said, introducing me to one such child. "She had a twin brother, but he died." I stare at the girl. "Twinny can sing just great!" says Mama enthusiastically. I am thinking of my years of piano and violin lessons with recitals that Mama attends by standing in back and sneaking out before it's over. I am remembering how she has never heard Georgie and me sing in harmony back at Vista Street, or in front of a whole church congregation when we were only 4 and 5, or seen me in the school orchestra sawing away on my violin in rapture as we play the "Pilgrim's Chorus."

"Sing that one you did the other night, Twinny," says Mama. And Twinny, in a coarse voice, imitating some torch idol of the day, belts out a pop tune. "Isn't she great!" says Mama poking me in the ribs and clapping. I am wishing that Twinny had died with her brother. Then I get the ultimate insult. "Guess what?" Mama says, "Twinny is going to spend the night. You can share your bed with her. You don't still pee the bed, do you?" They both giggle, while my cheeks flame red.

So, visits with Mama were not times of healing or reunion, but fraught with confusion. But still we visited, always on guard, more like observers than participants.

Her boarding house fairly hummed with eros and alcohol. Its residents socialized with one another, drinking, playing records and dancing while Mama Landlady looked on approvingly. When one couple's baby cried, I was asked to change the diaper and feed her. I was happy to be asked, because I identified with the neglected baby, alone in her crib. When the mother brought me the bottle, it was filled with beer instead of milk. "It'll make her go to sleep," the mother said. I knew this was very wrong, but dared say nothing. In the next room, a young man and his girlfriend were having sex with the door open. I knew that I would not tell Gram or my father about any of it and really had no way to integrate all these images. In my 12-year-old mind they were filed under Mama's Weird World, a place like no other, always. It was comparable to having a very disturbing dream. In fact, on one visit, as I slept, I was awakened by one of her drunken tenants attempting to rape me. I escaped by running to the bathroom and locking myself in for the night. She had left me alone in the house while she and my brother went somewhere for a late supper. Her understanding of vigilance and supervision had obviously not changed. Naturally, we were not allowed to visit Mama in that house again. And she no longer visited us either. The incident was never processed in my presence, but discussed behind closed doors by Gram and my father. Just as during her own pre-pubescent years, and during my mother's, Gram could accept sexuality only in the framework of marriage, entirely skipping over adolescence. Even though she had been brilliant in explaining Grampa's pictures of nude men to me earlier, she was now totally awkward regarding the incident at Mama's. So I went about my days in a cloud of shame and silence, when I desperately needed someone to tell me I was not at fault, and that my developing body was a healthy and beautiful thing. And, sadly, at the same time, our whole world was about to collapse.

chapter thirteen

Grampa's last wish

It was a raw and rainy October in 1943. The war still dictated many restrictions in our lives. No butter, no rubber, very little fresh meat. Grampa brought home a horsemeat steak one night from the North End open market. We all tried it and found it tough and gamey. Sometimes he managed to get some ox-tails for stew. Once, he brought home pigs' tails and Aunt Susie refused to cook them.

Our kitchen had maps of Europe, N. Africa and the South Pacific pinned up for reference. The radio news went on every evening to chart the progress of 'our boys' in this seemingly endless carnage and destruction. All movies started with a newsreel showing air battles, bombings and prisoners of war. Gram welcomed our questions and she and Danny, especially, would carry on long debates about political strategies, with him circling the dining room table in agitated determination to make his point. I drew cartoons of Hitler and Tojo, happy to diminish them to ridiculous icons. But Gram would speak of the Germans as a culture that produced great poets and composers.

"Schubert lieder sung by a choir of German men is some of the most beautiful music I have ever heard," she would say.

"But, I hate the Germans," I would counter. "They are the ones who started this stupid war. Hitler is our enemy. He is trying to come over here and bomb us too."

"But you see dear," she would say. "When we hate others, it is like holding on to a red-hot poker. It burns us, not the other person. Even though Hitler and the Nazis are doing bad things, not all Germans are bad. They are people like us. They want the war to be over too."

And she explained the Japanese the same way. They were fine painters and people of great aesthetic sensitivity. Even the Kamikaze pilots believed they were serving their country, just as our boys were. The wars were caused by leaders with selfish and cruel minds. They were to be pitied, for they did not know how to do right.

These explanations made it impossible for me to see in black and white anymore. I puzzled over the enemy being a person and the image of a red-hot poker became synonymous with hateful thoughts forever. Yet, she did not destroy my desire for the war to be over, or my belief that America was beautiful. I bought a war-bond with my dimes, clumsily knitted squares for afghans to comfort the wounded, noted the Gold Star banners in every other window as I walked to school, grew pathetic radishes in a window box for the 'war effort.' And I watched the campaigns in the kitchen, learning all the generals' names and the places of significant battles. WWII was not a distant abstraction. It was the primary topic of daily life in the 40s.

Grampa did an unusual thing that fall. He took a temporary job delivering bushels of apples for a peddler. He had to carry the heavy crates up many flights of stairs in tenement districts all day, until the truck was empty. He joked with Gram about how this would get him back into shape, since he had put on some pounds in mid-life. He bragged that the boss was impressed that a 65-year-old man could carry such a load. Gram became anxious that he was pushing himself too hard after some years of less physically demanding pursuits. But he was determined to bring home some much needed money and kept right on.

Because of chill rains in autumn, he often came home soaked through. Soon, he had caught a nasty cold. The cold evolved into a deep, heavy cough. Gram became more anxious and the old dynamic of Christian Science vs. medicine arose. The only antibiotic at the time was a compound of sulphur, and of course Grampa refused to take it. Then he began to have a fever. He refused to stay at home, but continued to go out each day and carry those apples up many flights. At night he was exhausted and having trouble breathing. Finally, he had to surrender and quit. It was such a disappointing, ignominious end to his endeavor.

He allowed Gram to make hot poultices for his chest to loosen the cough. No doctor was needed to diagnose his pneumonia. They both knew, but of course Grampa would not acknowledge it. The whole house felt sad and scary.

Grampa was unable to lie down now, and slept upright in the bedroom rocker. He could not climb the stairs either, so I would bring him little dishes of simple food and feed him. Gram made custards and Jell-O and he would manage one or two spoonsful before succumbing to a coughing spell. I wound up the Victrola in the parlor and put on some of his favorite records of hymns, then ran up to see if he was smiling. I kept waiting for him to heal himself with prayer, even repeating some of the Christian Science phrases he had taught me.

"Grampa," I said, sitting near him. "If you fill your mind with truth, there will be no room for error." He nodded, sadly, but did not show any improvement, much to my disappointment. I expected instant recovery with right-minded thinking. My opinion of Christian Science plummeted. It was not making my Grampa well, so it must not be true, I thought. And he was too ill to have a dialogue with me.

But he did tell me of a dream he had. I sat on the floor at his feet to listen, glad to have a distraction from my worries.

"I dreamed that I was in a room with beautiful Oriental

rugs," he said. "But as I walked on them, admiring their many colors, bright crystal flowers grew right up around me. They sparkled in the sun. I was very, very happy and delighted to be there. Then I woke up. I wish I could go back and stay there," he said, sadly. "Now I think I will try to sleep a bit, dear."

But shortly, he called out to Gram. "Annie, come here… please." They talked quietly. He felt terribly to be such a care, but was becoming agitated about needing to breathe better. In desperation, Gram suggested he go to the hospital just to get some oxygen. She argued that he should try oxygen, since it was a natural substance, not medicine. "You would be able to breathe so much easier, Louis," she begged. He finally agreed. She called the hospital and shortly, two ambulance attendants were carrying him down the stairs in the dining room chair he always sat in at Thanksgiving; the one with arms. Danny ran to him, smiling.

"Here, Gramp, you need this to cover your bald head," and popped his warm skating cap on Gramp, who managed a wan smile, before disappearing out into the cold November night.

Gram turned to us and said, "I will go with him. If I am not home in the morning, you will know he made it through the night. You girls can sleep in our bed. I've made a fire in the Franklin stove up there." She hugged us all. Danny said he would sleep in the parlor so he would know if she came home.

The Malden Hospital smokestack was a familiar landmark for us, just up the hill from our beloved pond and park. It was the hospital where Georgie had had her appendix out and where Danny had had his two broken arms set. Now, Gram walked up the long hill alone to be with her husband of 39 years as he struggled to live. She had seen pneumonia before and knew his condition was very critical. But, like every other challenge in her life, she faced this one with courage and calmness.

When she got to the hospital, Gramp was in an oxygen tent, as was the custom at that time. Even though his head was elevated he still gasped for air. She encouraged him to trust the oxygen to help. She found his strong hand and held it in hers. As she stood there, he turned to her and said, with great difficulty,

"Oh, Annie! How I wish...... Irene.... would come and..... tell me she...... didn't mean those....... those terrible things.... she said in... the courtroom."

This was a moment of intense distress for them both. Because Irene's accusations of him molesting her could never be proven or disproven. And although Annie believed she was lying and Louis had always denied it, such things can never be completely put to rest. The best thing would have been to call Irene and hope she would come and rescind her accusations. But, even if she could be expected to do that unlikely thing could she have reached the hospital in time? Had she gotten there, would she have been an agent of comfort, or distress? Annie must have considered all this and was not willing to leave her beloved's side to search for a pay phone. So, what might have happened to heal that wound can never be known. In my mind, my grandfather would not have been hoping for his daughter to take back her statement, unless it was a lie. In any case, he sought vindication even as he lay dying, for that was the last thing he said before he stopped breathing.

Now, Gram sat quietly for a short while, trying to absorb the enormity of the moment. Her long journey with the only man she ever loved was over. After a few moments, she walked to the front desk and informed the nurses. They offered to call her a taxi, but she said she preferred to walk. It was about 3 o'clock in the morning as she made her way back to Vista Street alone, numb and exhausted.

Danny met her at the door. She simply said, "He's gone."

She went to the parlor and sat down, put her face in her hands and wept. None of us had ever seen her cry, much less in a helpless posture. She was the one who stood tall, the strong face in the crowd at all our school events, always smiling and eager to watch whatever we presented. She was comfort when our foster parents tried to frighten us. She was the only one I ever heard speak authoritatively to my father when he acted badly. Now she was undone and needed strong arms, a shoulder to lean on. But all she had were three inexperienced children.

Uneasy and bewildered, Danny foolishly tried to make her laugh. "Now you're the 'Widder' Müller," he said. She did not respond and he new instantly that he had said the wrong thing.

Georgie had awakened when she heard the front door open and now came running back into the bedroom and jiggled me awake. "Grampa's dead!" she said with strange excitement, yet crying. I sat up, not knowing how to behave. I thought I should cry, but couldn't. I felt less sad than curious. I was wondering if I would get to see his body before burial. I had yet to realize how this dear man's absence would impact my life. I did not yet know the face of grief.

I remember no disruption of our days. Whatever crying Gram did happened while we were in school. She carried on as usual, except she was unusually quiet. Aunt Susie seemed dazed, her blue eyes often teary.

"My all-in-all is gone," she whispered one day as we met in the hall. I put my arms around her tenderly and she wept on my shoulder. She felt like a frail bird in my arms. Strangely, I could feel her loss keenly, but still was numb to my own. I had not yet shed a tear.

After a few days we were told we would stay home from school to attend the funeral. We put on our Sunday clothes, my sister and I in matching navy blue capes and blue felt bonnets. Danny squeezed into his one suit, already too short in the sleeves. Gram wore her black coat and hat with veil and Susie, a treasured mouton fur coat.

Mrs. White, our piano teacher, was to play the organ music and drove Gram and Susie in her car, while we three children walked together to a small funeral parlor downtown. It had formerly been some kind of shop with large windows, which now were covered with beige drapes. Folding chairs lined half the inner space and our former foster parents and two neighbors were already seated in the second row. They looked so solemn I thought they were cross, but Gram nodded toward them and we all sat down in the front row.

To one side was an organ. Mrs. White removed her coat and seated herself on the organ stool arranging her music. A grey metal casket stood close to the draperies and a bouquet of bronze-colored Chrysanthemums perched stiffly on a tall stool at its head. I strained to see Grampa's face, but only his perfect nose showed over the edge.

From somewhere behind us a stocky older man appeared and approached Mrs. White. They held a whispered conference then turned toward Danny. The man smiled and nodded at him, holding out his arm. Danny got up and stood beside the organ and the man disappeared in the back again. Mrs. White sat down and opened her music. She began playing the introduction, looked at Danny and he started singing in his young, sweet baritone voice.

"The Lord is my shepherd. I shall not want. I shall not want." I had heard him practicing at home. When he came to the part about the "valley of the shadow of death" his chin quivered, but he managed not to cry and finished with a confident crescendo of, "...and I will dwell in the house of the Lord, forever!" He sat down again and Gram patted his knee. All was silent. I wondered what was next, when suddenly the front door opened.

High heels clicked across the floor as Mama walked straight to the casket. No one moved to greet her, so we all sat still and watched. Rather than wearing a hat, Mama had tied a scarf over her hair, an echo of the Madonna paintings Gram had done of her so many years ago. She carried rosary beads, not discreetly, but prominently. In this setting they were a symbol of family wars and defiance. She knelt down and looked at her father's body for a moment. Then she made the sign of the cross, as Catholics do, and began reciting the rosary in an audible whisper. Those behind us didn't hesitate to comment under their breath.

"What's she doing here?" "Was she invited?" "I hope she doesn't cause a scene."

Finally, Mama made the sign of the cross again, touching her forehead, shoulders and heart with the cross on her rosary. She stood up from the kneeler, head bowed, back to everyone. Then she turned, her head held high, and clicked back across the floor and out the door. Gram sighed. I had a fleeting urge to run after my mother but sat still.

We were told that the casket was about to be closed and we were welcome to walk up and look one last time at Grampa. This is the part I had been hoping for. I examined his face closely for clues and saw nothing but a waxen image full of mystery. Grampa was not there at all.

In the following weeks I learned that his casket was buried in the Pine Grove cemetery where an empty space was beside him waiting for Gram. I had recurrent dreams of trying to rescue Grampa from some Gypsies that had kidnapped him and were hiding him in a cave. When I reached the cave, Grampa was there, but covered in moss. He was unable to come home with me. I told Gram.

"You see, dear, Grampa can't come home again. He is no longer in his body, but I believe that our spirits live on. And since 'love never faileth' we continue to love even after death. So, we can still love Grampa, and he can still love us, even though we can't be together for now. I think your dream is just about missing Grampa, which we all do, naturally."

After this explanation, I never dreamed of the evil Gypsy kidnappers or a mossy Grampa again. But I still hadn't cried.

School plodded on and Thanksgiving holidays were upon us.

Gram roasted a turkey, made her special creamed baby onions and buttery squash. I looked forward to the special Indian Pudding made in a crock passed down from generations to Amanda and Gram. Georgie loved green peas. Danny coveted the drumstick. He and Grampa had always claimed them. The white tablecloth was spread and a wonderful crystal dish full of celery stuffed with cream cheese and olives appeared. There were mince and pumpkin pies and cranberry relish, small pickles and cider in a glass pitcher. Aunt Susie put on her best dress with its lace collar and we all gathered around the dining table.

That's when I noticed his empty chair. The one with the arms where Grampa always sat. The same one that had carried him away just a few short days ago. And in that moment, his death became real to me. I pushed back my chair and ran from the room, up the stairs to the bedroom where my tears finally flowed. I now understood that he would never, never come home again. No one came up to interfere.

chapter fourteen
A subtle flaw

As winter wore on, it became evident that Aunt Susie was failing. For several years, Louis had been treating her for symptoms common to colon cancer. Now it was in its final stages. She and Gram agreed that she needed nursing home care. Susie believed she would die in the nursing home and was peacefully resigned to soon being with her beloved brother. Gram showed Susie great compassion through her last months, visiting her often and listening kindly always. It was on one of these visits that Susie pleadingly asked her, "Annie, could I be buried next to Louis?"

Susie was asking to be buried in Annie's wifely place. How many wives would have said yes? How many wives would have actually kept their word? How many would have refrained from spilling out anger, outrage, pent up feelings from years of insult and intrusion by this woman? But even though still in mourning, Annie was true to her life course. Unselfishness, sacrifice and kindness all came before her own feelings or needs. She thought only of how much it meant to Susie.

"Yes, Susie. I promise you that. I think Louis would have wanted you there."

"Oh, God bless you Annie. Now I can die in peace," Susie said, obviously very relieved.

Later Gram told me that she felt no regrets doing this, because 'poor, dear Susie had such a sad life and such a hard death.' She also said that she felt earthly remains should not be of much concern, anyway. She bought another plot for herself in the Abington Cemetery. Amanda and Tom, dear little Berty and Willie and her sister, Nell, would all be there with her. There was a certain resignation evident in this act.

With Susie gone there was still the question of three adolescent children to be dealt with. We were doing well in school. I was now in 7th grade, not behaving too badly, still playing violin in the school orchestra. Georgie in 8th grade, was chosen to sing at assemblies, Danny was a sophomore who also played clarinet in the high school band. But the area of Annie's great discomfort had arrived. Our emerging sexuality and its accompanying social complications were manifest. This certainly weighed heavily in coming events.

At the same time, she was getting fewer painting commissions. Color photography was eating into the art market and she had increasing difficulty paying the rent. That had been one of the reasons that Louis had felt he needed to take that fateful job just before he died. His death had taken a huge toll on her and she was simply worn out. She needed to simplify her life to survive financially, physically and emotionally. This would be the first time, as an adult, when she was not responsible for the care and well-being of others. If we no longer lived with her, she could move into a small apartment and survive on a monthly check from what was then called an 'Old Age Pension.' It was hardly enough for comfortable living, but if she could get an occasional painting commission to augment it, she would make this meager income seem like a bonanza. I have never met anyone who could stretch a dollar as far as she, managing both her bills and surprising little moments of luxury along the way.

Our mother was in dire straits, having been divorced by Harry upon his return home from Korea. He had had an affair with a woman in the Philippines that fell apart, and was now interested in unburdening himself of Irene. He had been in his early twenties when they met, and now was keenly interested in reclaiming his life. He was intent on using his GI bill to get a college education. He simply kicked Mama out of house with no money. She bravely got a job at a factory assembling electrical parts for GE. A kindly restaurant owner and his wife, rented her their spare room nearby and gave her one free hot meal each day. Her downward trajectory into poverty would eventually lead her to the House of the Good Shepherd, a shelter for homeless women. And even then as we heard of these things, they were told with scornful disrespect and total lack of compassion. She was blamed for her own fate. So we had little, or no contact with her during our teen years and lots of sad, bad feelings. I know that Gram must have suffered, as any mother would, to know her daughter was without shelter, sometimes without food, certainly without the love and support of any community of friends. Her beautiful Irene had ended up out there in the darkness and cold, all alone.

Our father had remarried. Josephine had been his personal manicurist and saw marriage to a doctor as a desirable step up the social ladder. They had bought a large house in Cambridge and he had started a new practice there. She was an excellent housekeeper and cook and they seemed quite contented. So, they were the logical ones to assume responsibility for the three of us.

As the school year came to a close, Gram told us we were going to live with Papa. Vista Street would be emptied of 39 years of memories that filled attic to cellar. We would go to Cambridge as soon as school was out to live under the roof of a father that had not raised us, or lived with us since we were 3, 4 and 6. We would intrude on a 10-year-old marriage that had no time, or experience with the daily needs of children. We would descend on a woman who was meticulous about order and privacy, whom we had met only once or twice in brief visits to Vista Street, where she openly expressed her horror at the chaos we lived in and loved.

"Dan, the girls have a squirrel in their bedroom!" she cried.

My pet squirrel, Nutkin, was perched on a curtain rod, dropping peanut shells on the floor. I had been eager to show her how he would come to me and climb up to my head if I merely patted my knee. Now I was afraid he would be taken away. But Gramp had found an old squirrel cage at a second-hand store and Nutkin was tucked in there for safety. Truly, our time of joyful indulgences like pet squirrels in the bedroom, magical Christmas stockings, story-telling, the music box and Gram's supportive presence was over.

"Mother Jo," as our father instructed us to call her, would have little interest in us except our usefulness to her. Their 12-room house housed Papa's office and waiting room, as well as four boarders. We would be taught to maintain sparkling floors and windows, dust-free baseboards and polished tables. The laundry, shopping and dishwashing would also be ours. Danny would maintain the lawns and Georgie and I would keep the rented rooms in clean sheets and vacuumed rugs. "Mother Jo," would enjoy chatting on the phone, playing solitaire and reading the latest novels, like *Forever Amber*. Conversation at dinner would usually include critiques and ridicule of other people, sometimes Gram or Irene. Or we would be discussed as though we were not present.

"Dan, give the girl some hormones. She'll never get a boyfriend with that flat chest."

"No, damn it. Hormones might screw up her menstrual cycle."

In short, there was no kindly interest shown in how we were faring, ever. After evening office hours were done, Jo and our father would disappear to their room and lock the door.

When I had first arrived, I had told Mother Jo that I did not yet know how to braid my hair. I assumed she would then teach me. Instead she said, angrily, "Don't think I'm going to pamper you like your grandmother did. I'll just cut your hair." Right then and there she got some shears and chopped my braids off. I stumbled up to my attic bedroom sobbing. I felt violated, because my braids were part of my identity. And of course my bed-wetting would not be tolerated, but ridiculed and punished again. I was unable to adjust to such radical changes and the loss of the only stable home I had known. I began to fail miserably in school and was not promoted. Papa called me into his office.

"I suppose you're proud of yourself!" he snorted from behind his huge desk. "It's a poor bird that fouls its own nest." I just stood there, shamed, tears running down my face, with no idea how this terrible downslide had happened. Nobody ever asked me how I felt, or what was wrong, or better still, how they could help. Thoroughly lost, I then developed a secret life, vandalizing, stealing and cheating in school.

How do I explain this to myself? After all I had had five years of unconditional love. Was all Gram's quality time and wisdom now lost? She had taken me in at 8 years, an unhappy, wounded child, and helped me grow into a reasonably happy pre-teen, close to my siblings, loving music, animals, the outdoors, school plays. I had actually liked school and did quite well. Why couldn't I carry my confidence and security with me? My sister and brother seemed to do it. But, perhaps because I was just at that very fragile moment in life when one moves from childhood into adolescence, I could not manage all the other changes simultaneously. Also, being the youngest, I had not had as much practice being in charge of myself. Danny usually told us what was going on, Georgie was always her own person and I was used to them telling me what to do. But now they were individuating as was appropriate. Our threesome survival group had disintegrated. So, my adolescence and young adult years suffered badly. Still it was mainly Gram's prudent interventions at crucial times that helped me avoid some of the worst outcomes. My father inevitably consulted her in every crisis.

I have no quarrel with being taught to clean, shop, manage my laundry, personal care and school responsibilities. Those skills should have been learned gradually as I grew. But, Gram had always been there to guide us in learning our lessons, memorizing lines for a play, working the math problem rather than assigning chores, just as she had done with our mother. Everything was done for us, lovingly, happily. I can only recall one incident when she made my sister do a chore.

Georgie found it difficult to sleep with me, as I would fall asleep quickly and breathe heavily. One night she decided to pinch me. I woke up crying, totally bewildered. Gram, trying to catch up on some cleaning, came in to see what had happened.

"I was asleep and Georgie pinched me awake," I sobbed.

"She was BREATHING, Grama," said Georgie, defensively.

"Well, if you can't tolerate your sister's breathing," said Gram, "you can get right up and help me scrub the toilet."

Georgie began to cry, horrified. She was fastidious and cleaning the family toilet was very low on her list. I even felt sorry for her. But Gram had a rare sternness in her voice, and Georgie did as she was told. It was one of the few times I sensed that Gram was really angry and at her wit's end. From the bedroom, I could hear it in her voice.

"I certainly would love to be able to sleep in a warm bed right now. But I will be up very late working. I hope you will now appreciate the luxury of sleep and better tolerate a little 'breathing' from your sister, Georgianna."

Needless to say, she did not pinch me awake again.

We were only vaguely aware that she never asked anything for herself, or took time to rest. She somehow didn't believe in children sharing housework. And that left our mother and us ill-prepared for what would be expected by the rest of the world. It is a blind spot in her that I can only explain by examining her own childhood experience.

I think it's quite likely that Amanda taught Nell, 5, to help out when Annie was born. As Annie grew, it was evident that she was an unusually bright child, which pleased her father immensely. Her attachment to him was evident in all her memories. Although she always spoke lovingly of her mother, it was her father that supported her prodigious memory, having her learn long passages and then recite them for his friends. Her only memory of him being cross with her was when she refused to recite for his friends once, when she was about 3. He made her sit at the top of the cellar stairs for a bit. It was her father who bought her the first box of watercolors before she was 8. She followed him around the farm as he worked. It was he who followed along with her college coursework later. And she most resembled the first son, Berty, who had been the apple of Tom's eye. While Amanda taught Nell more of the wifely chores as a matter of course, the 'baby' could trot around after Tom. Later, the girls' interests were different, in that Nell liked to sit with Amanda doing needlework, while Annie might read or paint. Her carefree, happy childhood was what she wanted for Irene and all of us. She did teach my sister and me to knit, crochet, embroider and sew clothes while we were still in grammar school, though. We actually wore the skirts and blouses we made to school, and slept in nighties we had sewn. But cleaning of any kind, except for Georgie's horrid little stint cleaning the toilet, was never encouraged. In fact, if we tried to get dishes washed, Gram would always gently lead us out of the kitchen. She did let Georgie try baking a cake once. With great effort she mixed and baked a rather pathetic vanilla cake. Since Aunt Susie was sitting in the kitchen rocker, Georgie offered her a piece. The cake had not really risen and had a coarse texture. Aunt Susie ate it politely anyway.

Then she said, in a toneless voice, "Mighty fine corn bread, Georgie."

Georgie was crestfallen, but Danny and I thought it hilarious, and this phrase, along with many others is still repeated with laughter in our family whenever someone bakes a cake.

In any case, what she provided to all of us, at such great cost to herself, was five carefree childhood years. They were the happiest of my entire childhood. But later, I tried to strike a happy medium with my own children.

I remember an incident when Gram was visiting my home after I had married. She and I were in the kitchen enjoying a cup of tea, when my small son came to us.

"Mummy, I can't reach my snowman puzzle on the bureau," he said. "Why don't you push your chair over and climb up and get it," I said, turning back to our conversation. He ran off and got his puzzle down easily. I thought nothing of it. But Gram was amazed. "I would never have thought to do that," she said. "I would have gotten up and gone to get it for him. What a clever girl you are!"

"Oh, Gram I'm not clever, I'm just lazy," I said laughing. "Besides it teaches him to be independent."

At the time, I was not making a pointed comment, because I hadn't yet thought through my own life with her. But her amazement, in retrospect, tells me that she hadn't realized how one can allow others to help themselves a little more, and therefore allow yourself to have time to rest. She had never understood that it was as imperative to say yes to her own needs as well as those of loved ones.

chapter fifteen
A new beginning

Alone at Vista Street, Annie faced the ghosts of her married life. The cellar was piled with Louis's inventions. There was the trunk with a box of letters she and he had written during courtship, Irene's tiny baby shoes, a curl of her hair tied in a pink ribbon, her porcelain doll, 'John' and albums of photos depicting her first 18 years. There were letters between Nell and Amanda about the antics of nine grandchildren, cards from Mary Levinia's Nova Scotian family, her elaborate hats carefully wrapped for special occasions, Aunt Susie's fur coat and everyone's sewing baskets overflowed with antique buttons from long-ago garments.

Slowly, she organized what might be of value, for she was without income. What was left of her last commission had to last until she was settled elsewhere. The landlord was extremely kind, having dealt with her for many years.

"Mrs. Müller, don't worry about the rent right now. You have always been a good tenant." She reluctantly accepted his offer, promising to repay everything as soon as possible.

She wanted very much to stay in Malden, so scoured the city for available apartments. There was no subsidized housing for low-income seniors at that time. She had to find an apartment that would cost no more than a portion of her old-age pension. Just as is the case today, it would be nearly impossible. But, she persisted until she came upon an eccentric, elderly man who owned a 4-family house. He did not favor upgrading his property, except to install electricity and paint the woodwork. Therefore, there was no central heating, no hot water, no baths or showers in his apartments. One kept warm by lighting the oil-burner in the kitchen stove. One took a sponge bath at the kitchen sink, heating teakettles of water on a small gas range. And in the unit Annie was offered, one went carefully down very steep cellar stairs to a dirt cellar to use the toilet; a genuine water closet, its water tank overhead for flushing. It was similar to Vista Street, which also had no hot water and a coal stove in the kitchen. But, this was in the mid-forties when nearly everyone in urban areas had tubs, showers, hot water and central heating. Yet, Annie was thrilled, for the rent was just $23, one quarter of her monthly check. To put this in perspective, an up-to-date 3-room apartment in a good neighborhood at that time, might rent for $45.

Maple Street, where her new home would be, was close to the downtown train station and her beloved library. There was a small grocery and fish market right around the corner. Her apartment had a very small front and back yard to be shared with the tenant upstairs.

There were three rooms in a row. From the front porch and hallway, she entered a medium sized bedroom. Next came the middle room with an outlet for her Franklin stove and an inside wall for the piano. A small back hall and on to the kitchen with a window on two sides and access to the cellar toilet. Annie was completely satisfied and very grateful to have found this, her new home.

Back at Vista St., she still had a sturdy wagon that we had used to fly, screaming, down a nearby hill over and over on summer days. It had slatted removable sides to increase its capacity for hauling things. Each day she would fill it to the brim and pull it all the way across town to Maple St. as many times as she could manage. Then, she would select some item of value and take the train to Boston to barter with antique dealers she had contacted.

"One day I had nothing at all left in the pantry," she told me later. "Then I remembered the antique buttons. I packed them up to take to a wonderful button shop on the corner of Boylston St., not even knowing if they would buy them. I had only my carfare in change. But I went to Boston, absolutely positive that I would sell them and have enough money to buy my supper that night. And I did! I got home just in time to go to Buddy's Lunch for a pot of steamed clams. Sometimes we have to simply go on faith."

On some days Danny went over to Malden on the bus to help her haul, but otherwise, she actually moved nine rooms into three nearly all by herself. The final move of piano, bed and a few other pieces was done by a moving company, paid for with dollars she had laid by for that purpose. And even when she had no food, she had not touched them. For to ask anyone to lend her money was not even a consideration. She actually was invigorated by the challenges of poverty. Always thinking around obstacles to find a way to get what she needed or wanted, with very little money. Call it frugality, or Yankee ingenuity, she was the master of the old adage, 'Use it up, Wear it out, Make it do, Or do without.'

She was now living alone for the first time in her entire life. At 65 she was in reasonably good health, as far as she knew. But, what was creeping up on her was failing eyesight. Her optometrist had told her she was developing cataracts and therefore could expect some cloudiness. She attributed this to age, and started reading with a magnifying glass. Nothing was going to hold her back from the luxury of reading and studying all the things she had been looking forward to for so many years. Her days were hers at last. And she filled them with reading and building a garden.

As she was busily tending to weeds in the front yard, a gentleman walked by several days in a row, saying good morning as he passed. One day he stopped and spoke to her. They exchanged greetings, spoke of the weather and he introduced himself, asking her name as well. She was polite, but kept right on with her gardening. He lingered.

"Say, Mrs. Müller, may I ask what you do for excitement?"

She turned and faced him. "Oh, I stay as far away from it as I can. Now good day, Mr. X."

Remember the little boy with a May Basket who got his face slapped? And dear Alan in high school who sent her a sweet love note in Morse Code? That same Annie was still alive and well at 65. No one was going to steal her privacy and solitude ever again.

The garden had been neglected for years. Previous tenants had thrown coal ashes out there and except for some well-established weeds there was no greenery. Annie saw this as a great project and rolled up her sleeves to dig. Very soon, the upstairs neighbor, Mrs. Parker, was calling out the window.

"That's where I'm putting my tomatoes," she said. "That's my side."

"Oh, I didn't know that," said Annie. "I'm only trying to get the soil turned. There's a whole lot of hard ash here. Do you mind if I try to turn your side too? Then we can both work our garden beds more easily. I think it would be nice to have a little plot of grass too, don't you?"

"I'm not going to bother with all that," said Mrs. P. "I just want a few tomatoes. I guess I don't mind if you fix it up as long as you don't plant on my side. I'll put up a string so you'll know where the line is."

Next day, Annie went out to find two sticks with a string tied to them planted well over the half measure of the miserable little plot. But rather than find fault with this action, she saw it as funny.

"When you don't return provocation, it stops," she said. "You can't punch a pudding." She continued cultivating the soil, hauling in loam in her cart, planting grass seed on her 'half.' As the tender green blades began to appear the contrast with Mrs. P's side was even more outstanding. She planted her tomatoes against the back fence, while Gram began gathering some wildflowers for her borders. Blue chickery, daisies, ferns for shady spots and buttercups. She frequented the local 5 & 10, which sold small shrubs and potted flowers in spring. Often they were not watered carefully and looked limp, about to die. She would take them to the counter and convince the clerk that they should be marked down—perhaps even given to her to rescue. Very often she would come home laden with scraggly, neglected things she'd bought for a dime, convinced that she could get them well. And, yes she did. Before long her garden was a joy to behold.

Heavenly Blue Morning Glories covered an arbor she built herself near her back door. At a nearby construction sight she talked the carpenters into giving her all their scraps of lumber and imperfect bricks. Scarlet runner beans climbed the trellises she built and white lilies bloomed profusely along the brick walk she laid. A window box held pansies. A climbing yellow rose nearly covered her kitchen window, breathing its fragrance with every summer breeze.

By this time, she had won over Mrs. P. to the point that she let Annie have the whole yard. Mrs. P. gave up on the tomato war and declared that the grass was like velvet and liked walking out there to hang laundry. Neighborhood children soon discovered the 'Flower Lady' and came often to visit for a bloom to take to their mothers. One of these children became a particular favorite. His name was Dickie Gordon.

Dickie was alone often, as his mother needed to work, and his older brother tended to go off with friends. Gram always welcomed him, but was concerned about his welfare. She went to visit his mother to tell her what a very fine boy he was, and probably to assess his home situation. Dickie was perhaps pre-school age when they met, and she remained friends with him until he was grown. Later, when she had moved away, he contacted her.

"I just want to thank you for everything," he said. "I did so well in school I've been accepted at University of Massachusetts," he said. "And, Mrs. Müller, it was because of you. You taught me so much and I am very grateful. My brother didn't do so well. He never finished high school and ended up in trouble. But, I had you, and that's what made the difference. All the time in school I would ask myself, 'How come I know this?' and I would remember, 'Mrs. Müller taught me that.' "

Once, when I was visiting Gram, I remember Dickie coming to visit when he was about 9. We had just sat down to lunch.

"Hi-ho, Mrs. Müller!" he called.

"Oh, dear, it's Dickie," said Gram, going to the back door. "Hello, dear. I can't talk to you now because I'm having lunch with my granddaughter," she said kindly. "Can you come back later this afternoon?"

"I just have to tell you one thing," he said with great excitement.

"All right. Just one thing," she said laughing.

"Remember when you told me the earth was turning around every day?" he asked.

"Yes, of course. That's what makes the night and the day happen," she answered.

"Well, that's not true!" he said. "I can prove it. Look!" And he jumped up as high as his little legs would propel him, and landed. "See?" he said, jumping a second time. "I was looking at you when I jumped up and when I landed I was in the same place. So if the earth was turning, I would have landed like this!" With that, he jumped and twisted mid-air so he landed with his back to her. "See?" he said, triumphantly. "That's how I would have landed if the earth was turning."

Gram stood there smiling. "Dickie, look how well you thought that out. When you come back later we will talk about it again. Thanks for showing me. Now run along, dear."

I thought about how she had filled my days with that same kind of encouragement and intellectual exploring, where learning was real and now and so much fun. What a blessing for all who met her as teacher.

So, she gradually found her place in this new neighborhood, making friends with her landlord, the grocer, the man at the fish market. He would give her the lobster bodies, usually thrown away, for 10 cents each. With careful picking, she could glean enough meat for a great salad, enjoying it more than anyone in an expensive restaurant.

At the library she joined The Great Books Club, an adult forum for reading and discussion. Very soon, she found the leader and some of the other members to be compatible friends. Not that she wanted to socialize, or go to their homes. But she now had someone to share ideas with and that filled her need to be with others at times. She exchanged pleasantries with the other tenants, but otherwise was very contented to be alone.

One afternoon, after doing errands, she rested on her bed in the front room. It was a balmy day and her window was open, curtains moving slightly in the breeze. She heard the tenant on the first floor opposite her come out to the porch. Some chairs were set out, and two women began to chat. Annie was drifting into a nap when she heard her name mentioned.

"So what do you think of your new neighbor?" said one voice.

"Mrs. Müller? Oh, she's alright I guess," said the other. "But I don't much like her, though."

"Why?" said the first voice. "What's she done now?"

"Oh, she ain't done nuthin', you know," answered the other voice. "It's just that she's too sweet to be wholesome, I say. I don't trust that kind. Too sweet to be wholesome."

"I know what you mean," said the second voice.

Annie could barely keep her laughter quiet. Instead of being hurt, she thought this was one of the funniest critiques she had ever heard. She told all of us about it and it became a family joke. When any of us do something really nice, we still tell them they were too sweet to be wholesome. By laughing instead of taking offense, she demonstrated again, that 'you can't punch a pudding.' If Gram wasn't teaching with words, she taught by example. You could not be around her for very long before you learned something valuable for your own life. She was the first one to make fun of her own failings, always. A rare kind of humility that did not diminish her personal dignity one bit.

chapter sixteen

Still my angel

World War II had ended. From my attic bedroom in Cambridge, I could see the crowds celebrating on Massachusetts Avenue, stalling the trolley traffic, holding up their fingers in a V. I felt grateful for the end of fighting, but horrified by the reports of Hiroshima, Nagasaki and Nazi concentration camps. Unlike Vista Street, there was no family discussion available. I had to sort out my feelings alone and felt as though I were in mourning for the whole world as well as my own life. And my life was not going well at all. I had failed Algebra and Latin and had not been promoted to 10th grade unless I could pass both exams in the fall. So far no one talked to me about possibilities.

Then suddenly, I was told that Gram had offered to tutor me. In spite of my father's feeling that she 'spoiled' us, he never hesitated to consult her when we presented him with a problem. So, they had decided that I was to go live with her for the summer. Still disbelieving that I could ever pass any exams, my spirits rose ever so slightly at the thought of being with Gram again. She had had just two years of freedom before I landed back in her lap, wounded and lost again. What kind of summer was this to be for either of us?

I should have remembered that what Gram always said was true. She had written on the blackboard at Vista Street, "Love never faileth." And she lived by that truly. She made me feel completely welcome. Not once did she chide me for failing. She made the summer ahead sound like a grand adventure where she and I would overcome every obstacle. She started out by setting a schedule for study and tutoring, with free time each day for fun. She bought my favorite foods, as though we were having a party.

"Dot, dear, I know you love watermelon and can never get enough of it. When we are through today, I am going to buy a half melon and you can eat the whole thing yourself if you like." And I did.

I don't remember one unpleasant day that summer. I don't remember hating the work and study. All I remember is flash cards with Latin vocabulary, declensions in her beautiful hand. We read the text aloud to one another, translating as we went. She would insert Latin words into our conversations. Algebra became like a puzzle, instead of a horror show. She gently made it clear how y could end up equaling x squared. It was as though the pages in my schoolbooks had been written in scrambled alphabet before and she had straightened out the words. It all made sense now and my confidence grew proportionately as the summer progressed.

In the afternoons we had picnics, library visits and craft projects. She taught me how to make papier mache and model some marionettes. With scraps of cloth she showed me how to hand sew costumes for them. I built a marionette theater out of a wooden box and wrote a play. Mr. Libby, Gram's landlord, let me put it on in his barn. I was so happily engrossed I didn't care that there was an audience of only two. I still have one of those marionettes. Cambridge, my disastrous school failure, my father's scorn and Jo's disregard were far away. None of my delinquent behaviors surfaced all summer. I was home and safe with Gram.

When fall came, back in Cambridge, I walked into the high school principal's office alone to sit for two comprehensive exams. I remember feeling completely calm and assured and aced them both. Would that have happened if Gram had not been willing, once again, to sacrifice her plans and all that time for me? I believe I would have sunk even deeper into my personal hell. The timing was crucial. No one else could have done what she did so effectively. She knew exactly what I needed and made sure I got it, no matter what the personal cost to her. Surely, a very troubled teen, who is failing in school and acting out badly, is not what most people would choose for their summer pleasure. She was a miracle worker. An angel.

When I was very young and first became aware of her in the world, I realized she was my lifeline. I decided she must never die. I knew angels did not die.

"Gram," I said, "you are an angel."

"Of course not," she said laughing, "I'm just fat old Grama who loves you."

I kept on insisting until she realized what was behind my statement. Then she talked to me about life after death, our souls living forever and how "love never faileth." We would have many, many conversations about this throughout my lifetime, and even now, still do.

Now that my promotion as a sophomore was secured, my father had another surprise for me.

"Come on," he said, with rare friendliness. "We're going for a ride." I thought he was going to make some house calls. So I got my coat and was ready to go.

"Comb your hair and stand up straight, for God's sake," he said crossly. I did as I was told and got in his latest shiny car, a green Hudson Hornet. We drove a long way in silence. I wondered about the inconvenience of a patient living so far away. He pulled up at a drugstore in a strange city outside of Boston. We went in and he ordered two Cokes. I should have been a bit suspicious, because he never took me anywhere like this, and certainly had never bought me a Coke before. He downed his quickly and told me to hurry up. We drove on in silence. Finally, we entered Wellesley Hills, a pretty suburb west of Boston. He slowed down and turned in at a tall iron gate, up a winding path toward a Gothic brick building. He parked the car.

"This is called The Academy of the Assumption. You'll like it here. When we go in you keep your mouth shut."

We rang the bell, which was answered by a nun in black habit with terra cotta beads at her waist. She led us through gleaming corridors, dimly lit by red vigil lights. I walked on my toes so my loafers would not click on the shiny stone floors. We sat in a large room with oriental rugs. My chair was so big that my feet didn't reach the floor. The first nun smiled at us and disappeared through an inner door. A second nun appeared and shook hands with my father. She introduced herself to him as the principal, Sister Rose Catherine. Then she looked at my bare legs, bobby sox and penny loafers in silence.

"Our girls wear stockings," she said, quietly. I pulled my legs in under the chair as far as I could. She and my father talked for a few moments. I noticed him trying to make jokes with her, but she didn't laugh. She handed him some papers and we were ushered out the door.

Back in the car, he let loose all his pent up fury at having to spend money on me because of my behavior. And then he launched into a diatribe about Roman Catholics, the Popes and the nuns and the "God-damned" Catholic church.

"All they want is my money," he yelled, veins on his neck pumping out. "Did you see those Oriental rugs? They have plenty of money, those bastards."

I knew better than to speak. Instead, I studied the papers Sister Rose Catherine had handed him. It was all about the Academy. There were lists of things I would need to bring. A navy blue blazer, white blouses, 6 pairs of stockings, brown oxfords, black slippers, a silver setting for meals, a Catholic Missal and rosary beads.

Some might think I was terrified to be sent to this convent boarding school; to be under the aegis of those my father despised, and about whom I had heard Gram and Grampa say negative things. But, instead, I was excited. I was going to get out of my father's house and be in this fascinating and mysterious cloister with the soft-voiced nuns and their intriguing rosaries. It would be years before I would understand that everything about the convent drew me because it was connected with my lost mother. She was the only person I knew that had rosary beads and acknowledged the Madonna, a universal symbol of motherhood.

And why did my father choose this path for me? Frankly, he was at his wit's end. My secret delinquencies had been discovered and failure in school was the last straw. The nuns would straighten me out, he thought. In fact, when he was growing up, his older sister, Beatrice, was sent to convent school as a matter of course. Beatrice had not been a delinquent girl at all, nor was she Catholic, but convent school was considered a safe haven for young ladies then, to keep them chaste before marriage. He assumed that my next disaster would be pregnancy, even though I had never even been on a date. But, perhaps he was remembering my mother's fate (for which he was heavily responsible). So I was tucked away where there were no males.

My friends gave me a going away party and looked at me with wonder and admiration. For the first time in my life, I was to be separated from my siblings. I would have a new identity as the only Protestant at the Academy; one to be converted, to bring glory on whoever convinced me to abandon myself to Catholicism. And how my classmates and I debated! But, in spite of my strong opinions, I fell in love with the ritual, the rich colors and sensory stimuli of incense, candles, Gregorian chant. The long periods of silence were healing; my rosary beads fascinating. I longed to be a saint, even a martyred one. I decided to become a Medical Missionary of St. Francis as soon as I graduated. Weekends came and went, and I stayed at school, enjoying long walks with girls who were from abroad and the more lenient atmosphere allowed on weekends. Just before Christmas, Mother Jo called.

"Your father wants to know when you're coming home," she said. I explained that I had no money for a bus and was all right at school. No offer to come get me was made, or course.

"Well, we will send you enough for the bus," she said. "You should come home for Christmas at least."

I reluctantly packed my bag and made the trip through Boston to Cambridge, arriving late afternoon. I felt as though I had been away for a year. No one met me at the door, so I went up to my room to wait to be called to dinner.

The house seemed garish, too ornate. No dimly lit spaces with flickering candles. Voices loud and rude as my sister and I sat beside one another at the kitchen table. I made the sign of the cross and whispered a prayer of thanks, not even thinking how it might appear to these 'strangers.'

"Guh!" said Papa, using his corrupt word for God. "Who are you? Little Miss Holy Holy?"

Flustered, I explained that we always said grace at the Academy. Georgie, trying to lighten things up, said, "What I want to know is if the nuns wear black underwear."

This made Papa laugh and the conversation turned away from me. But I realized that my new sense of the sacred in prayer was a joke to them. I decided not to reveal any of my plans to study for my confirmation and first communion, and I certainly would not say anything about becoming a nun.

Each day I got up at 6 and took the trolley to early Mass. When I passed others on the stairs at home, I stepped to the side as the nuns had taught me. And I couldn't wait until Christmas was over and I could fly back to my haven. As I left for the bus on the last day, Papa went to the door with me.

"Make sure to say hello to Father Away for me," he chortled, obviously very pleased with his joke.

As usual, all my 'disturbing' behavior was reported to Gram. In fact, my Aunt Beatrice was called for a family meeting about what to do with me. "I loved convent school," said Aunt Beatrice. "It never hurt me at all."

"She's acting so holy it turns my stomach!" stormed Papa, pacing the room. "Those Papist hypocrites have got her in their clutches, now. Making that cross sign right at my table. Going to church every damned morning, as though we were dirt. I won't have it under my roof. She's going back to public school next year. Bring her back to her senses."

"But Dan," Gram said in a soothing tone, "look at what she has accomplished. Everything you had hoped for. Good manners, good grades, behaving beautifully. She's made a complete change for the better in just half a year. How can this be a bad thing? Many young people are turned around by a religious experience, you know. Couldn't it be so for her? If she had a chance to continue in that environment it might be just the thing she needs to do well. Right now she is exploring Catholicism. Later on she may explore other ways of thinking. I wouldn't worry about Dot. I think she has the ability to think things through for herself."

Once again, Gram intervened in my behalf, making a huge positive difference in my fate. I was allowed to continue at the Academy. And as I moved through the stages necessary to complete conversion, Gram was my oasis, the only one who even tried to understand. I would, in my naivete seek to explain dogma to her. She never tried to dissuade me, only asked interesting questions. She actually accepted my invitation to attend Mass once, and afterward, patiently stayed to hear my version of the Stations of the Cross around the sanctuary. I felt heard and comforted in my search for something to anchor my storm-tossed life. Her tolerance for my zealousness was saintly considering the fact that Catholicism was a religion she did not favor. Later, I would revert to my earlier roots taking with me all the beauty and truth I had found in orthodox Christianity.

But at that time, Catholicism and convent life gave me the assurance and stability I desperately needed. Without Gram's intervention I would have been stripped of all of it.

chapter seventeen

Irene reinvents herself

In her beloved three-room haven, there was no room for a proper studio. But Annie would not let that stop her from painting. The kitchen had sufficient light during the afternoons. So she set up her easel there and completed a commission from one of her calendar companies, Brown & Bigelow. It was her least favorite topic, that of a toddler doing adult things. This baby was seated at an office desk with a pencil behind his ear, holding the telephone askew as though he were making a business call. The colors were drab to begin with. But, Annie now found that she needed to intensify the tones before they looked right to her. Although her drawing was still fine, the finished painting had none of the signature lightness that had made her watercolors so attractive. She expressed frustration and disappointment when she showed it to me. Even I could tell that something was terribly wrong. Although Brown & Bigelow still accepted and paid for it, they didn't ask her to do another one. So, fifty plus years of painting in a competitive market ended in her early 70s. She began sorting through unfinished works that were her own, such as the Greek bust, and the painting called "Elegy." Now, since they were nearly complete, she was able to finish them. She was asked by a friend, to paint a poster-like work showing the signs of the zodiac. She truly enjoyed this completely fun and original project, painting something she had a strong interest in always. Also, a grand-niece asked her to do two small watercolor portraits of her children, which she completed nicely. And as far as I can recall, these were the last paintings she did.

By this time, Danny had graduated, enlisted in the post-war Navy and went on to Middlebury under the GI bill. Georgie was commuting to the Boston Museum School of Art and I was at the now defunct Lynn General Hospital School of Nursing. Our father had suffered a heart attack and recovered physically. But, after about 15 years of not drinking alcohol, he had resumed where he had left off. His behavior became typical of what we like to call, "mid-life crisis." He dyed his hair and neglected his practice. He inquired of me if any of my fellow nursing students would like to date him. And he made the fatal mistake of getting involved with one of his female patients. This last behavior, when discovered by Jo, actually precipitated a psychotic break in her. Here she was, finally free of Danny and me, with Georgie very busy at art school and her husband was dissolving in alcohol. Her dream of resuming their peaceful life before our arrival was shattered.

Confronted with her extreme emotional distress, Papa's reaction was true to form. He did not change his behavior, but managed to get her committed to a mental institution. While she was hospitalized, he divorced her. This was not legal even in those days, but, remember, he had spent a lifetime gathering judges, lawyers and policemen as buddies, and he succeeded. He then told all of us to get our stuff out of his house, or he would throw it away. What little I had was in my bedroom closet. A very worn Teddy bear, one precious doll, my glasses from first grade, a pumpkin pin I won for best Halloween costume and some precious old books. Since I was unable to leave school and take the long train ride home to get them, they were tossed in the trash can. The house was sold. Papa rented his bedroom and office space from the new owners, who became drinking buddies with him. None of us visited him more than once in this bizarre setting.

And where was Irene at this time? Still living in her room above the restaurant and working at the factory. But, an interesting man had decided to befriend her. His name was Salvatore Lombardi, called Pete. He was an uneducated first-generation Sicilian widower with a two-year-old son. Just out of the Navy, he worked for the Massachusetts State Highway Dept. He lived with his parents, who cared for his child in their East Boston apartment. Directly below their living room, was a fire station, where howling engines careened out into the streets at all hours. His father was very ill, and lay on a cot in the kitchen, while his mother, Concetta, made the daily pasta and marinara, hanging homemade pastas to dry over the backs of the kitchen chairs. She went barefoot and spoke no English. Pete's child, Tommy was disciplined by having objects hurled across the kitchen at him. Often he would hurl them back. If I were to visit my mother, it would have to be here.

Concetta seemed pleased. "Eat, eat!" she would say, smiling and nodding at me, as she put huge bowls of food at the table. My mother would nod too, indicating that I'd better do as I was asked or insult Concetta. Of course, this was Mama's favorite environment. The one she had always sought out as soon as she was in the upper grades of grammar school, people who lived simply, were generous and had a strong sense of family. This was really our first genuine connection since being separated. It was a connection because I enjoyed it as much as she did. She enjoyed letting me in on her world. It was refreshingly relaxed, as Mama was not trying to deal with her feelings around her parents here. And, more important, I was not expecting her to take me in her lap anymore. Nobody cared about furniture or clothing, or whether the dishes were cracked, or who had custody of whom. And the food was luscious.

Pete maintained his distance. He was courteous, but did not engage in conversation. However, he would make comments directed at me. Although I saw his living conditions as poverty, he saw them as having everything.

"We were never poor," he told me. "We always had enough to eat." The fact that he never had a pair of mittens as a child, or music lessons, books and trips to museums was irrelevant to him.

Other statements came from his belief that all mothers were like the Madonna.

"Youse should respec' your mudder," he would say sternly, if I said something he didn't like. When my boyfriend dumped me, he sat beside me, and looked at me with deep kindness in his eyes.

"Der's plenty of fish in the sea, dearie," he said softly, seeing a tear on my cheek.

Later on he would take Mama and me to the empty race track parking lot on a Sunday.

"Here," he said, handing me the keys to his car. "Youse is gonna learn to drive." Mama sat in the back seat, while I lurched and stalled around the lot, with Pete calmly instructing me.

"Slow down! Hit the brakes!" he cried as I approached a gate. I slammed them on, tossing Mama to the floor. He did not yell at me. Mama started to giggle as she sat up.

"I'm going to get a shiner," she said. "I whacked myself on the door handle." Sure enough her eye was turning a rich purple and blue color. Instead of complaining or blaming me she laughed.

"Come on," she said. "Let's go down to that photo booth on the beach and take my picture!" That was a typical example of how my mother reacted to such things now. As though everything was a lark. Pete's steadfast presence seemed to allow that for the first time since I had known her. So, though I was now homeless, as she had been, I had a place to visit, besides Gram's, that was welcoming. And Pete turned out to be a permanent fixture for the next forty years, always treating me kindly. Of course he was critiqued by my father.

"Look how far Irene has fallen. A Sicilian street worker," he would say, never realizing that Pete was a far better man and father figure than he had ever been.

From her more secure base, Mama now approached Gram cautiously, introducing Pete to her. Gram worked hard to find nice things to say about this man who was so far off her charts. But she never criticized him. And he treated her with respect, because she was Irene's 'mudder.'

One May, on Mother's Day, Gram received a phone call from Irene, who had now resumed calling her 'Mother' instead of Madame. Whether or not Irene now believed Annie had given birth to her was not clear, because no one ever discussed what had happened in the courtroom. Why upset the delicate détente that now existed? It seems that Pete's reverent attitude toward Madonna/Mother figures was having a positive effect at least.

"Hello Mother," said Irene, "Pete wants you to come on a picnic with us and Concetta since it's Mother's Day."

Annie was astounded and flustered, as she had no expectation of this sudden burst of friendliness. She had not met Concetta and still felt somewhat ill at ease with Pete and Irene. To spend more time with them on their terms pulled her way out of her comfort zone. Yet, to her credit, she said yes. What a difficult thing it must have been to put herself in the company of a daughter with whom no truce had been declared, no apologies ever made, no verbal reconciliation even approached. But she would not refuse the possibility of overcoming their wars. 'Love never faileth; forgives all things.'

She prepared some egg-salad for her sandwich and tucked green grapes and a thermos of lemonade in a basket as she waited for them to pick her up. Pete came to the door, carried her picnic basket for her and even took her arm. Annie usually refused such conciliatory help, but now she simply thanked him. Pete would have paid no attention anyway, because this was simply how one showed respect for one's mother. He seated her in the back beside Concetta, with a very brief introduction. Since Concetta could not speak English, she simply smiled a nearly toothless smile at Annie, and they were off.

Irene was somewhat aloof, talking only with Pete in the front seat and giving Annie very brief responses over her shoulder as she attempted conversation. They finally pulled into a wooded parkland. Pete helped Annie again, and Irene walked ahead with Concetta. When they reached a clear place under some pines, Irene spread out a blanket and they all sat down. Pete opened a very large cardboard carton, setting out cold cuts, crusty bread, olives, potato salad and a bottle of red wine with paper cups. Concetta looked at Annie. "Eat, eat!" she said enthusiastically. But Annie took out her familiar fare and laid it on a small towel instead, indicating that she had brought her own lunch. Irene lit a cigarette and turned her back on the mother as though she were annoyed.

"When in Rome, do as the Romans do, Mother," she said, between her teeth.

"Help yourself," said Pete, looking at Annie's Spartan lunch. "We got plenty."

After they had finished eating, Concetta got up and wandered off through the trees. Annie noticed she was barefoot. Irene and Pete watched her disappear.

"Youse should go wid my mudder," said Pete. "She's gonna pick some mushrooms."

"Oh, how interesting!" said Annie. "Irene, do you remember how you and I went with Papa to pick mushrooms? You know, Pete, Louis was a mycologist and I still have one of his wonderful books identifying edible mushrooms. Perhaps Concetta would like it, since I don't collect them any more."

"Oh, Mycology, Piecology, Mother," said Irene curtly, "Concetta doesn't need any books. She's been doing this all her life, even in Sicily when she was a little girl."

Stung by her rebuff, Annie remained silent, and finished eating though she had lost her appetite. Pete packed the leftovers back in the car and he and Irene decided to take a stroll leaving

Annie on the blanket. She got up and walked by herself, trying to make sense of her unease. And so the afternoon passed with this undercurrent of disdain from Irene, Pete bravely maintaining his cool, and Concetta oblivious as she happily gathered her mushrooms. When she brought them back, cradled in her apron, she poured them out on the blanket for all to admire. With horror, Annie spotted a Deadly Amanita lying there.

"Oh, my," she said. "I'm sure that one is poisonous. You see the little web under the cap? It distinguishes it from the..." but before she could finish, Irene rudely interrupted her.

"I told you Concetta knows what she's doing. Why do you always think you know everything? She could teach you a thing or two about a lot of things besides mushrooms."

"My mudder knows mushrooms," Pete said, stretching and yawning. "I t'ink we should be goin' home now."

When they drove up to Annie's apartment, Irene said goodbye without looking at her, but Concetta smiled at Annie. As Pete escorted her back to her kitchen stairs, Annie took one more chance.

"Pete, could I just give you that mycol...mushroom book? I am so worried that your mother may have picked a deadly one."

"Nah," he said. "She don't need no books. My mudder knows her mushrooms. Don't worry."

Annie entered her home, set down her basket and sighed. What had been accomplished? Certainly no greater peace between Irene and herself. No relationship with Concetta. How does one relate to people like Concetta? Her only comfort was that Pete was a gentleman, in his own way, and now she could make herself a cup of tea and recuperate from the whole ordeal. Mother's Day.

During the following Christmas season, Pete's family gathered for a feast. Concetta had made brajole, raviolis, meatballs and marinara and a roasted turkey. She decided to bring out a jar of her mushroom marinara from the previous fall, as well, but no one wanted any of it except her. Everyone was eating and talking when suddenly Concetta collapsed at the table. They rushed her to Boston City Hospital. She was pronounced dead; poisoned by a deadly mushroom.

"Yah, she croaked right at the table," said Irene as she informed Annie the next day. But did Irene ever make the connection? Did she apologize to Annie for not respecting her opinion? Did she admire Annie's astuteness, or ever stop to adjust her assumptions about her? No. It would always be so between them, as though Irene was eternally stuck in the place of adolescent disdain for her mother's very existence. And Annie had the grace to say nothing about the fatal picnic.

Pete's work took him out of the Boston area. He bought a mobile home. He was promoted to a superintendent's position with the state highway department. He became a specialist in dealing with bridges. He and Irene were invited to dinners for state politicians running for election. And his loyalty to Irene never waivered. She was a Lombardi now.

After Concetta's death, Pete's extended family had gathered from several New England states to decide the fate of his son, Tommy. Before and during his birth Tommy had suffered some brain damage. It manifested itself in mild seizures, cerebral palsy affecting speech and serious learning difficulty. His early years with Concetta had not enhanced his language skills and by the time he was 8, it was recommended he be placed in an institution for mentally disabled children. Because his mother had died right after giving birth to him, Pete had never been able to separate the infant from her untimely death. Tommy was at fault, in Pete's book, irrational as that may seem. He had no interest in raising him and left the matter to his relatives. On the weekend of this gathering, the family could see no solution but an institution. After all had left, Mama and Pete noticed that Tommy was missing. They hunted through the house and finally found him in an eaves closet in the attic. Mama scolded him.

"What are you doing in there? We've been looking all over for you. Now come out!"

Tommy folded his arms over his chest and shook his head. "I ain't comin' out. I want a mudder."

"Aw, gee, Dot," said Mama when relating this story. "What could I do? The last thing I wanted was this kid. But I couldn't see them send him to an institution for life, could I?"

And so Tommy became her kid. An 8-year-old whose father didn't much care for him, who had many hurdles to overcome just to be marginally independent later on. A prospective mother figure who had a child-rearing philosophy that in the kindest terms could be called unique, or laissez-faire. My mother whose heart had been broken over and over, who had protected herself with fantastic explanations for her disasters that never seemed to include her own behavior and choices. Tommy was a very needy child and now Irene came face to face with his daily care. Pete was a help only in providing a consistent male presence. He was yet unable to show any interest or affection to the boy, but would exert his authority in a few words when necessary. The schools that had already rejected him showed little interest in providing suggestions for his education. Certainly they would not let him back into the classroom at this time. Fortunately, Pete's job required a move so Irene could enroll him elsewhere. She began by fudging his records. So Tommy got his day at school, for better or worse, and when he got home to the trailer, Irene would tutor him until suppertime. He managed to get by, day after day and complete the year somewhere near the bottom of the second grade. But that was progress. And now Irene and Tommy were a pair, both aiming at beating the system.

To illustrate how Irene operated when she was championing a cause, consider this. One of Pete's brothers was married with five children. He worked in a donut shop and supper might be only stale donuts, some orange soda and a piece of bologna. His youngest child, Anthony, had suffered developmental damage due to meningitis as a baby, and spent his days on the street shining shoes. He was a sweet child who took Irene's heart. His siblings and other children, however, often ridiculed his prominent ears, calling him Dumbo. No amount of talking could dissuade them.

It was common in those days to remove tonsils and adenoids routinely, thinking to reduce the number of infections most children get. So these five children were all scheduled for surgery at Boston City Hospital. Their mother was timid, so Irene agreed to go with her to deal with the doctors. A young resident had been assigned to do the surgery. Irene asked to speak with him alone.

"You do some pretty wonderful things with plastic surgery nowadays, don't you," she said. "See that little boy over there?" She pointed to Anthony, across the room. "The kids hurt his feelings all the time. They call him Dumbo. He's never going to be able to go to school or anything because of the meningitis, but everyday he shines shoes and gives the money to his mother." She paused a moment to let this sink in. Then she sighed. "Poor kid. If only he could have that operation where they pin back ears like that. Do you think that while you've got him under for the tonsils, you could do that for him? It would change his whole life to have the kids stop making fun of him all the time, you know."

And lo and behold, when Anthony awoke, he not only had a very sore throat, but his ears were bandaged. When they had healed, the surgeon gave him a mirror. Dumbo no more. He smiled and said, "Wow! Look, I've got new ears," and his mother cried with joy.

This was the beginning of Irene's 'social work' career. She had found a way to use her untapped abilities to help those around her. She knew poverty first hand. She cared deeply for those who suffered without recourse. And even though she had no formal education after high school, her intelligence now had a focus. Everywhere she looked, around the trailer park families and in

Pete's family, there were those that were less fortunate. And she was moved to help them.

To educate herself, she called hospitals for recommended literature on brain damage. She sent away for books on educating learning disabled children. She made up games that kept Tommy from giving up in frustration. Scrabble worked well for learning to read. Chess for critical thinking. Vocabulary flash cards pinned all over their small space. And constant tutoring.

Tommy needed help with social skills. So, she enrolled him in Cub Scouts and became a Den Mother. Now the trailer bulged with energetic young boys soaking up cookies and her firm but welcoming ways. Tommy learned to take turns, to share, to compromise in disputes.

Shy mothers would tap on the door and ask if she could teach their child how to read. Her growing confidence led to theories that supported her brand of wisdom.

"After the tying of the shoes is learned," she liked to say, "every child should learn to play chess and make meatballs."

That statement still makes me smile because I doubt any other mother or teacher would ever have come up with that intriguing combination. Lots of wisdom but with a special quirkiness that wakes you up. A good-natured challenge from someone on her own island. Irene was never dull.

As she studied more, she learned of a simple test done at birth that could detect a disorder, Phenylketonuria, that left untreated, could cause serious brain damage. With a special diet for the first few years, a child could outgrow it. She soon became the official tester for her whole trailer park, detecting two children that had left the hospital undiagnosed. She was fully engaged, intellectually stimulated and accomplishing things that an experienced nurse or dedicated social worker could be proud of. And this allowed her to approach Annie with a different attitude. For now she could stand in her own territory of success.

Their conversation became basically all about Tommy's progress. Annie was truly amazed and greatly pleased to see her daughter making such an important difference for him and so many others. She listened patiently to Irene's daily lessons with Tommy, which were related sometimes with great humor. And Annie accepted, without a murmur that Tommy was now to be called her grandson. She bought him books as he progressed and always treated him with the kindness that children drew from her nature. So, in the odd way of the universe, much healing took place during these years. Ironically, Annie, who had made the difficult decision to testify that Irene was unfit to raise her own children, could now genuinely praise her daughter for parenting Tommy so well.

When Pete was hired to help build the air base at Limestone, Maine, the family moved from their city trailer to a rustic farmhouse in Fort Fairfield. It had a well, an indoor 'outhouse' and a woodburning stove for cooking and heating. Irene saw it as a grand adventure. She and Tommy both worked harvesting in the potato fields with their neighbors before school was in session. A cattle farmer next door taught Tommy how to muck out stalls and say, "Bullwhacky."

At night the wolves howled and owls hooted. And then there were many barn cats and their kittens. Irene wrote copious letters to her mother about all of this, her humor and rich imagination flowering as she described a mouse that crept out of its nest behind the stove each night to taunt a kitten, Curiosity. Curiosity had fallen off the roof and whacked his head, she said, making him a bit slow to catch this rascally mouse. And she continued to share her novel educational style with her mother as well. She demonstrated beautifully that her careless disconnect with her biological children had matured into a dedicated, attentive relationship with Tommy. And in her letters, Annie caught glimpses of her good-natured adolescent Irene, who had so enjoyed a rustic summer cabin in

Bath, Maine with her so long ago. For Annie this was something to rejoice about, however bittersweet it was. She passed on all Mama's news to us even though, at the time, we were all embroiled in our own life dramas, and could hardly appreciate the import of this time of detente between them. Speaking only for myself, I was relieved that my mother was no longer homeless. And I cautiously liked and trusted Pete. But I was not yet mature enough to embrace the idea of Tommy as my 'brother.' Instead, I was envious of the mothering he got that I had never known from her.

DOROTHY NYMAN - '71

Irene at 63 years, life sketch by author.

chapter eighteen
Déjà vu

G ram could feel some contentment that Irene was safe and well, after years of poverty and jeopardy. Pete loved and respected Irene and she was productively engaged in good work. But Gram's contented solitude was to be interrupted in the late 40s. Although she kept on taking her Harvard courses, corresponding with her daughter and tending her lovely garden, all three of her grandchildren were in crisis. Since Dan had sold the house and turned his back on any further responsibility for us, we could think of no one else to turn to but Gram.

Georgie, in her 4th year of art school and winning honors, now had nowhere to live and an upstairs apartment in Gram's building became vacant. It was similar to hers in that it was a cold-water flat, heated by a kitchen oil-stove, and had no real bathroom except a toilet in a hall closet. The rent was $28 a month because it had another, unheated room in the attic. Georgie got a job at a small retail store and could manage quite well there. So she moved in, using her bedroom for a studio and slept in a small alcove to the side. Problem solved.

Then Danny, about to enter his 3rd year at Middlebury, was in crisis. A sweet girl he had fallen in love with, turned him down. On top of that, his pre-med courses no longer interested him. He became anxious, then despondent, then suicidal. Fortunately, he came home to Gram to sort it all out. Together they walked around the beloved pond near Vista Street, talking through his tortured response to disappointment and confusion. It became clear that he did not want to return to Middlebury, but needed time out. So, Gram gave him her bedroom and placed a small cot in the kitchen for herself. She told him he could stay as long as he needed. Shortly, he found a therapist and started studying jazz piano with a great teacher, practiced for hours and at the end of the year was hired as fill-in pianist in several Boston nightclubs.

My crash was equally devastating. Unable to process my father's drinking behavior and heightened callous disregard for my needs, I became terribly depressed. When he trashed my belongings and told me to find somewhere else to live, I didn't have a clue how to manage all that. I went underground again, as I had when I first went to live with him, acting out in secret delinquent ways. On the surface I was a hard working senior student, but inside was extremely depressed and completely isolated. Occasionally, I would call Gram crying uncontrollably and she would attempt to shore me up to no avail. I simply did not have the inner stability to endure more chaos. When I was discovered stealing, my supervisor promptly expelled me 28 days before I was to receive my diploma. No help was offered to a student that had given three years of dedicated labor and was one of the top three in her class academically. What was to become of me now? I had lost my nursing career, had no employable skills except typing and was too undone to imagine any happiness ever again. Of course I turned to the only one that had ever been there for me.

Gram suggested that Georgie sublet her attic room to me.

"No!" she said. "I don't want her living with me." I can hardly blame her. What sister that's just managed to solve her own problem wants the burden of a total basket case sibling? But Gram continued to pressure her, lecturing about kindness and selflessness until Georgie agreed. Thank heavens for a roof over my head and Gram right downstairs. Now all of us were together again in this hodge-podge arrangement that gave Gram little privacy or rest.

But as troubled as we were, Gram again helped us to remember that it was love and kindness, selflessness and gratitude, joy in small things, that made for happiness. She convinced us that we would come through and move on, that we were lovable, capable young people.

She cooked our meals and we contributed money. That allowed us frequent meals together in her small, cozy kitchen. We paid for her to go to a local boarding house, weekly, where she could have a refreshing hot bath and 24 hours respite from the 'sturm und drang' of our lives. It probably prolonged her life and we were greatly relieved that she allowed us to reciprocate for the first time.

During that terribly crucial year of oasis, Gram encouraged me to join her at the Great Books Club after my workday. She paid for me to take ballet at the Adult Education Center, something I had always wanted to do. When Danny enrolled at BU, she encouraged him to read aloud from his texts in an early English Lit course, and her kitchen became a place of laughter and happy discussion again. At art school Georgie had studied the great masters, replicating their techniques exactly until she shone as a classical artist. Gram was greatly admiring of her ability throughout, until Georgie began experimenting with abstractions and expressionism. Even though it was a necessary part of her studies, Annie could not abide deviation from the ideal form. It was difficult for them to find common ground. One painting in particular was a very large portrayal of the historical event of the Children's Crusade, wherein the subjects were wan and purposely distorted, in the style of El Greco. After much futile explanation and heated discussion Gram made the comment, "I suppose it has to be ugly." Granted, she had tried very hard to understand the theory behind distortion. But like Freudian psychology, Annie resisted new interpretations of things she held sacred. Greek idealism and realism in art could not be improved upon as far as she was concerned. She did accept the Impressionists, but stopped there. Just as truth was not relative, neither was her concept of beauty. And so, there was disagreement between them regarding art. The effect of this did not dim their love for one another, and Gram posed for many student drawings and several excellent interpretive portraits still. But Georgie did not have the unconditional kind support she might have hoped for. One might wonder if two factors were at work in this instance.

The painful reality of being unable to paint at all, might have been sharply brought to mind as Georgie shared her exciting new studies. She had not only the luxury of sight, but the opportunity to paint what interested her instead of honing her work for a commercial market. That might have made Gram's plight more painfully present. In any case, she was not happy being at odds with those she loved and often tried to talk it through, but this gulf never really got resolved. After her fifth and final year, Georgie was awarded a travelling scholarship and went to Europe to continue her studies. Upon her return she moved out and opened a Boston studio with one of her former teachers. They were married a few years later. I am sorry Gram did not live to see the mature works of my sister. One of her achievements was being commissioned to paint official portraits of the Federal Supreme Court Justices for the N.E. School of Law, which would have pleased Gram greatly.

In any case, the year of our difficulties passed eventually. Danny got an apartment in Boston and supported himself, eventually putting himself through law school with his now superb cocktail lounge style of piano playing. No longer relegated to small bars as a 'filler,' he had his place in fine hotel lounges.

I worked as an office assistant for a kind physician who allowed me to act as his nurse even without my diploma. That was helpful in pulling me out of my despondency, but I could still imagine no future for myself, except to find someone to marry me. Within the year, a widower with a 4-year-old son was my husband. For better or worse I had a home and a purpose.

And now Gram could breathe easy. Irene was settled with Pete and raising Tommy, and all of us were managing our lives well. There would be no more intrusions in her little apartment, only visits with new babies. I was the first to bring her a great-grandson, David, whom she called "a merry little fellow." My lovely daughter, Julia, followed. Then Georgie birthed Judith, Benjamin and Abigail. At last, Danny joined us and fathered Robert, Emily, John Michael, Helen and Daniel. Georgie's son Benjamin would become a professional artist.

Dorothy, Daniel & Georgie 1952

Gram, 75, with her first great-grandchild, David, son of the author.

chapter nineteen
Finally, liberal arts

During the 60s the Cold War squeezed the world. Anti-American rhetoric poured out of Russia and anti-communist rhetoric poured back from America. Gram's favorite nephew became a peace loving American Communist. He and she loved debating Communism vs. democracy every chance they got. He was nevertheless on Joe McCarthy's black list and lost all his commissions as a respected sculptor. When Gram heard of an organization that was seeking American teachers to write to Russian teachers as a peace effort she joined. For several years letters flew back and forth from Malden to Moscow. Her Russian pen pals were two teachers who taught English. Each one explained their view of the United States, heavily influenced by Communist propaganda. They believed that a capitalistic society would not support their elderly or poor. Gram cheerfully responded with descriptions of her apartment, lobster salads, book clubs and free medical care. Some of their letters came through with large segments cut out, similar to the censoring during WWII. They exchanged photos of their families and became very congenial, finally, which was a small success at the grass roots level in undermining propaganda tensions. Gram truly enjoyed describing democracy and defending the USA, but always with great diplomacy and care. She was a cradle Democrat and especially admired Eleanor Roosevelt. She and Danny had loved discussing the elections even when he was in elementary school, as he had a great interest in history and politics.

But now, alone, she was free to explore more affordable opportunities to study. The Centers for Adult Education in both Cambridge and Boston offered wonderfully rich courses, and the Great Books Club in Malden continued to be enjoyable. But, she was looking for something deeper and even more challenging. She discovered that Harvard University offered full college curriculum through its University Extension. This program was funded by the Lowell Foundation, which stipulated that each college credit could never cost more than the price of a bushel of wheat on the common market. It may be still that way. In the early 50s that meant about $5, or $20 per course, as they were each 4 credits. Each course lasted one year, with the semester break in January.

Harvard faculty was augmented by professors from MIT, BU and other area universities. There were no entrance exams given. You simply enrolled and if you passed the course, you were given your credits. However, if one was to matriculate credits, they must take more than half of their courses with Harvard faculty. Requirements, were quite flexible. Two courses in English, two in a foreign language, two in science/math, two in history. The remainder were student's choice. When enough credits were earned, a diploma with a BA in Liberal Arts was granted on the same platform with regular Harvard students. For one who had postponed gratifying her desire for more formal education for decades, this was a great boon. Thanks to the Lowells' foresight and desire to serve everybody, even her small income could take her to Harvard. And so she started feasting at the table there and would continue for nearly twenty years.

She explored psychology extensively, but found Freudian theory offensive. His focus on the importance of psychosexual development rather than the development of character through broader experiences quite annoyed her. And to top that off, he used her beloved ancient Greek hero, Oedipus as the archetype of familial incest. Yet she continued to search for answers to her own life, especially her relationship with Irene, through the lens of psychology as well, without much success. If she enjoyed a professor she would take every course he offered.

Other subjects that she studied deeply were those on scientific theory of the time. Had Steven Hawking been alive, no doubt she might have written him a letter of inquiry on one of his books. All the great philosophers were on her card as well. She was probably happier during those years than at any time in her life. Transportation was not a problem, for the Boston train station was only one block away. Once in North Station she could find her way to Harvard Square easily on the subway. This was crucial as her sight continued to dim.

"When I come home at night after my classes," she told me, "I open my little gate into the garden, look up to the stars and say, 'Oh, thank you, thank you!' It is such a rare privilege to study what I have been wanting to for years and years with the finest teachers in the world."

There was nothing to disturb her studies now and she began thinking about her own theories as they related to the great minds in her texts. She became fascinated with the idea of finding a unifying theory underlying all creation, as had many before her. She studied philosophers and physicists who expounded on this particular idea and finally began writing her own theory. Although I can't do justice to what she was formulating, some brief excerpts from her notes may show the reader what kind of thinking engaged her even in her eighties.

HYPOTHESIS OF TRINITY

1. Every unit of quantity, in other words, every finite form, is a state of qualitatitive trinity. Or, to state it in another way, every unit of form is three-dimensional in quality.

2. This is necessarily so, because at any point three relations to its environment inevitably exist. If we consider a

primary point existing in an infinite field, then these 3 qualities arise as attitudes between that primary point and the infinite field. Here, the trinity of quality is an infinite trinity, for nothing exists to limit it. Every finite form is 'identified' by a focal point of integration at a definite level of complexity in the progressive evolutionary sequence.

3. The three qualities may be designated as focal (+) radial (-) and (+-), the combination of both, which is at the same time, neither.

   In the infinite aspect this (+-), or median term is obviously identical with the unqualified matrix within which the other two are differentiated. Here, the (+-) is also infinite and may be visualized as an infinite plane, or surface where + and − lie in conjunction.

4. In the evolutionary emergence of finite forms, each successive complexity includes its simpler antecedent. E.g., the atomic form includes the primary form, which is 'light'—electro-magnetic energy. The three-dimensional mass of matter includes, is composed of atomic forms integrated on a new level of complexity. Vegetation is an integration of material masses (colloidal molecules) on a new level.

She wrote the above, clarifying ideas that fascinated her, but more importantly, to provide logical structure for her reader. We all write with our readers in mind, and hers were the professors that she had engaged over the past 20 years in her classes, as well as the authors of all the texts from which she had drawn understanding. When speaking of such things, her intense focus was electric and her power as teacher was evident in every illustrative example. It is no wonder that her professor had introduced her as "one of the most elevated minds he had been privileged to know." And it is no wonder that many people felt awed, or found her difficult to relate to. It was a thorn for Irene, as well, who in later life, arguing with her mother, called her a moron before slamming down the phone. Gram reacted a little out of character in this instance. She actually went to a psychological testing center and came out with her IQ score and sent it to her daughter. It was 180. I, for one am glad she did that, for it would be easy for me to exaggerate Gram's attributes out of love and gratitude. She couldn't help being brilliant and suffered the consequences.

For about two decades she earned many more credits than she needed to graduate, always an A student and the joy of her professors. Her record came to the attention of the administration as well.

"Mrs. Müller, if you would matriculate your credits, we would like you to join this year's graduating class as our honored guest. We invite you to be the representative of the School of Extension Studies to demonstrate what a student can accomplish here."

Rather than being flattered, Gram was not even attracted to the idea. "Why, I don't need a degree. I study for the love of it. It would not be sincere on my part to accept your offer, although I thank you," she told them. They were very disappointed, as was I. I longed to see her being honored, but my less admirable desire was to be able to boast that my grandmother was a Harvard graduate! I would have happily shelved the adage, "Pride goeth before a fall," to brag about that. But, Gram, in her eighties at the time, more than deserved to do as she liked. And there were poignant reasons that she did not want to be held up as an example. She was certainly not a typical student and never had been. And her earlier experiences of social ridicule for being scholarly were never forgotten. She preferred to remain anonymous.

The years of scholarly pursuit and freedom from the care of others.

chapter twenty
Fall into darkness

When she was 85, one evening Annie walked from her apartment to mail a letter and leave some breadcrumbs for the pigeons at the nearby train station. As she started back across the street, a young man in a hurry, sped around the corner and his car struck her at about 40mph, actually running over her leg.

She lay unconscious in the gutter with a severe concussion, a shattered left upper arm, dislocated thumb and fractured pelvis. At the hospital they placed a rod, a plate and some pins in the humerus and reset her thumb. Although she was grateful to be alive, she was heartily annoyed that her record of never having swallowed pain medications had been broken. She was told that she probably would no longer be able to raise her arm over her head. One of her nieces brought her to her home in Abington to recuperate. By the end of the summer, she proudly raised her arm way over her head, of course.

But, now the agency for the blind made the determination that she could no longer live alone. She was told she needed to be within walking distance of a family member willing to look in on her daily. She begged them to let her return to her apartment where everything was familiar. They said the steep stairs to the cellar toilet were too dangerous. She even demonstrated how she could scoot down the stairs sitting down, but they were not moved. Had she not been struck by a car and come to their attention, she might have slipped under their radar for years. She knew the neighborhood, the neighbors knew her, shops were nearby and she could navigate her three rooms even in the dim light of her encroaching blindness. Most important was the fact that she had been very happy at Maple St. sanctuary for nearly two decades.

I wish I could say that all of us who loved her were skilled and experienced in assisting her through this crucial time, but none of us had any experience to guide us. Now an octogenarian myself, I know that maintaining my independence is crucial. My children would never dream of making decisions about where I am to live, or what to do with my belongings. I feel free to discuss these things with them and consider their respectful suggestions. They offer support and encouragement always. How fortunate for me! But, sadly, we treated our beloved Gram quite differently. It is painful to admit that we did not afford her a serene passage through her last years. We blundered badly.

Firstly, we addressed the edict that she must live within walking distance of a relative. To our surprise, Irene and Pete offered to be the people that would oversee her needs. Perhaps believing that our mother was capable of viewing Annie as needy and dependent was our first error. Underneath the thin truce afforded through the medium of Tommy, wars of the past still simmered. Irene would always see her mother as a potential enemy. Annie would always question the truth of Irene's accounts. And there was the terrible accusation about her father lurking forever in the shadows. There was too much unfinished business for the total trust she now needed. Yet, we all foolishly accepted Mama's offer, pooled our resources and bought a small house in Revere near the trailer park where Mama and Pete lived. Even that was a disaster. The house was perched on a steep hill, with steep stairs. It had no yard, no shops, bus stops or library nearby. Not even a place to mail letters. Gram would be pinned in its strange rooms trying to feel her way around, all alone. Only the telephone could keep her connected with the outside world. And very soon it became clear that, although Pete dutifully delivered her groceries, Mama had no intention of ever climbing the hill to look in on her. There would be no visits, cups of tea or comforting assistance, only a daily phone call. And these calls became increasingly disturbing for both.

Prior to her move, while she was still recuperating at her niece's home, we had cleared out her apartment. Without consulting her, we blithely tossed out what we decided was unnecessary, giving her no chance to say goodbye to many of her belongings. We had no idea how callous and hurtful this was until she lamented the loss of her favorite old teapot. Even then we couldn't empathize, thinking it had been high time to replace it with something less dented. I am happy to say that we carefully moved her books and paintings, at least. That is some comfort.

Danny and his new wife and baby decided to move in with her until they could afford another place. It seemed to be a good idea for all.

But, of course, it was not. Gram was required to accommodate three other people now. Danny's new wife was kind, but had no idea who Gram was or what kind of history she had stepped into. The only positive thing may have been that the baby cheered Gram, and she had someone with eyes to help her acclimate. They all made the best of it, strange as it was, but after a few months the young family was able to move out and Gram was finally alone again, for better or worse. True to form, she simply struggled to make the best of it, blamed no one, still tried to laugh at the absurdities. She must have been terribly lonely, as none of us visited often, thinking we had resolved her dilemma by moving her into this small hell. How ignorant we were.

It was not until we got a call from her in terrible distress that we became more aware of how inappropriate her situation was. She had suddenly suffered from acute angle glaucoma, an extremely painful condition. I took her to the Mass. General Hospital and it was decided that she must have the affected eye removed. Her suffering woke us all up to the fact that we needed to do much, much more for her. We realized we had placed her in dangerous and unacceptable isolation. Now we behaved a little more sensibly. We all offered to take her into our homes. After much consideration, she chose my home in Abington, probably because she knew and loved the town. With some help from her pension, we were able to add on an ample bedroom, with room for her desk, a small kitchen unit and private bath. She felt relieved to be in the town of her youth, where some of Nell's children still lived. It looked like an ideal solution at last. I was very grateful to be able to care for her and have her company. My husband was cooperative and kind as well.

Our children were 8, 11 and 15 and very soon discovered that they had a private tutor in residence. Assigned Shakespearean plays with their difficult language slowly became understandable. The algebra x's and y's made sense. Gram, even nearly blind, would simply hear the problem and the child would sit beside her at the desk and work it out with encouragement and clarification. After school, there was another pair of ears eager to hear about my children's day. And at supper, she could join us or manage her own meal quietly alone. I felt really happy to be providing her with comfort and security. And our priceless conversations about life could continue. At the time, I was studying advanced piano with a fine teacher in Boston, and Gram enjoyed listening to me practice the same repertoire that my mother had. At birthdays, she could still see a glow from the candles. She still dreamt in vivid color. She managed to memorize her room and use her small stove to cook her favorite pork chops and make her tea. Her blindness was a lesson in compassion for all of us, especially since she bore it so bravely.

One morning, while preparing her breakfast, she dropped her orange on the floor. Rather than ask for help in retrieving it, she crawled in a grid-pattern all over the room, determined to catch the beast. Finally, after about an hour, she came to my kitchen.

"Dot, dear," she said, obviously tired and frustrated beyond patience. "Could you help me find my orange? I've been crawling around for an hour and can't get it!"

The thing had rolled under her bed, where only a broom could sweep it out. But she had entered into the search with curiosity and a sense of play, almost. I had never seen her defeated before, and by an orange, no less.

There were times when I could hear her reciting long poems aloud, or talking to Louis about their marriage, or to Irene about their unfinished business. She would exercise her body by walking round her room or lying on her bed and doing bicycle motions with her legs in the air. Public radio discussions sponsored by the Boston area universities were a rich source of interest. But, her days were long and it was hard to find things to quench her thirsty mind. Books on tape would have been wonderful for most people, but that resource focused on classic literature, while Gram wanted cutting edge physics and philosophy. We finally located, through Catholic Charities, a volunteer who was capable of reading her choices to her. It was a lovely woman, Miss Stillman, owner of Ocean Spray Cranberries, who faithfully read for several years and became fast friends with Gram. Occasionally we would invite recommended clergy for some theological discussion with her. But we never found rabbi, minister or priest who was erudite enough to survive their first encounter with Annie. None of them had the eclectic approach she favored, or the ability to quote from such a variety of sources. I think even the Pope would have floundered facing her questions and theories.

Occasionally she would be called by former Harvard professors, hoping she would join them in an upcoming seminar at MIT.

"I'm sorry, I can't. You see, I'm 90 now, completely blind and nearly bed-ridden."

After a moment of silence, the caller would stumble out an apology and say goodbye.

"If only I had my eyes! There's so much I want to know. I want to know!" she would cry, pounding her fists on the bed.

She told me sadly one morning that she now realized that she was no longer dreaming in color. Everything was black and white and very dark, even in sleep. Her world was becoming increasingly void of everything she had cherished.

chapter twenty-one

Death by courage

Georgie began visiting regularly and encouraged Gram to record her thesis since she could no longer write. They spent many afternoons engaged in this endeavor, giving Gram much needed diversion from loneliness and total frustration. Danny visited with his children and Gram's physical health, though frail, was good overall, except she began to have trouble swallowing. Nothing alarming, just a nuisance, she said. Georgie took the last photograph of Gram sitting by the window of her bedroom in her bathrobe. Her expression in this portrait captures poignantly the painful reality of her situation during that time.

For some years I had been pursuing a college degree and had enjoyed sharing my studies with Gram after she came to live with us. My children had now all become teenagers and I was able to take on a good number of piano pupils. It was the first time that I had moved beyond the role of housewife/mother within my marriage. I had some money of my own and was making new friends at school. I had the goal of becoming a professional psychologist. All of these things were positive events for me. But not for my husband.

As I spread my wings, he became increasingly unhappy. Although I continued to manage my home and help him in his business, he could not accept the change in our previous dynamic. His model of marriage was as a traditional patriarch with a totally subservient wife. He could not accept me as an equal partner. I suggested marital counseling, which he hotly rejected. So I began therapy by myself and as I continued to grow, my marriage crumbled further. I could not foresee how seriously this was to affect my ability to fulfill my earnest wish to care for Gram. I felt not just a moral obligation to her as a frail elder who had cared for me, but wished to finally give her what she had given others so selflessly all her life. I expected to nurse her at home until she died in her own bed, surrounded by love. These were my intentions.

But, her death was to be like every other major transition in her life. It would not be serene, but would come to her in solitude, among strangers, after a tortuous journey.

Our oldest boy graduated and joined the Coast Guard. Our second son began to flounder in high school. We couldn't agree on solutions. The strength of every marriage, I think, is tested sorely while parenting teens and ours could not survive. My husband and I became strangers and then enemies. Always with a volatile temper, he now became dangerously abusive, controlling and threatening.

I avoided revealing any of my problems to Gram trying to believe that somehow we would get through it. But finally it was necessary.

It was required by the state of Massachusetts as a prerequisite for divorce that one party had to leave for six months. It would have been easier for all if my husband had been willing to leave, but at the time there was no way to negotiate with him. So when I had to tell Gram that a divorce was imminent, she simply could not understand my reasons. Suddenly I was gone, leaving my home and children.

Danny offered me sanctuary during the six months. I arranged meetings with my children as often as possible without my husband's knowledge, as he had forbidden it. I was also forbidden by him to visit Gram. When I spoke with her on the phone, she had decided that I was 'so like Irene' in my behavior. I had not dared to share with her how terrified I was regarding my husband's violent threats. He had become very disturbed, threatening to kill me, the children and himself. I was praying just to get through the six-month separation in hopes that he would accept the situation with reason eventually. I just wanted to return home alive to resume caring for my children and Gram. Meanwhile, he maintained an entirely different persona with Gram and was being his kind self to her. It was a bizarre situation for all, happening at the most unfortunate time for Gram and my children. Yet for my safety and theirs, I felt I could not do otherwise.

About two months after I had left, Gram's swallowing troubles increased enough to require medical attention. It was determined that she had a slow-growing tumor wrapped around her esophagus. She would need either surgery to remove it, or a feeding tube in her stomach. She refused both ideas. I was excluded from all discussions about what to do, and she was placed in a nursing home near Georgie.

The home administration placed a feature article in the local newspaper announcing the arrival of a 'famous artist, Annie Benson Müller to be the guest of...' their facility. They took a picture of her in her distress, and interviewed her about her painting career in a bizarre attempt to sugarcoat reality. Everything they did violated her privacy and her wish to simply die in peace.

"Oh, Mrs. Müller, we are honored to have you with us, we hope for a long time," they said.

"I certainly hope not!" she retorted. "I hope this is over very quickly."

Mama called her often. Unfortunately, and predictably, even as her mother lay dying, she was not able to relate appropriately to her. All the accumulated pain between them roiled up unhappy discussion of things that would now never be finished. Noticing how these calls distressed her, the nursing home staff asked Gram if she wished to have her phone disconnected. She sadly agreed.

Of course, that meant that no one else could call either. I visited once, fearing rejection, since I still could not fully explain to her why I had needed to leave when I did.

She lay curled on her side, many pillows around her, rumpled linens over her thin, pale body. I bent over and kissed her cheek and told her I loved her. She said she was uncomfortable and I offered to rearrange her pillows to support her back. She accepted my offer. So, without speaking of the issue between us, I tucked and smoothed, loving this small moment of grace. I was doing what I had longed to do for her.

She said, "Oh, there now, that feels so much better. The nurses never seem to get it right. Dot knows just how to do it!"

We talked a little about how her days were long and she wished them to be over soon. And I asked, "Gram, are you afraid?"

"Not at all!" she answered. "I am in the hands of a loving God. I have no idea what comes next, but whatever it is, it's all right."

Georgie was able to visit her daily. On one visit she felt a surge of sadness and exclaimed, "Oh, Gram, you have had such a difficult life!" "Nonsense!" Gram retorted. "I got every lesson I needed!"

Even under those terrible circumstances, she harbored no self-pity or blame for all the disappointment, betrayal and utter frustrations she had faced throughout life. She viewed the pain as her failure to grasp the lessons she had been given. And she viewed the lessons always as given by a loving God in whom she had absolute faith and trust. She had always talked openly about death and dying, and continued to do so now. She and Georgie made a pact that if it were possible Gram would contact her after she died.

Even at 92, her general health had been good, so she lingered day after day, unable to eat or drink anything. Though she refused all medicine, and IV's, taking only tiny ice chips to moisten her mouth, she survived for nearly a month. Essentially, she died the very hard death of thirst and starvation.

On the last night she asked, "Could you give me something to help me sleep?" By morning she had left her body.

Her wishes were for a simple graveside funeral at the Abington Cemetery. But even here, she would not receive what she hoped.

Because Irene was her daughter, she was able to claim Gram's body. Her aim was to give her a wake and Catholic funeral. Nothing could have been more representative of the chasm between them. There lay Gram, surrounded by Pete's relatives, rosary beads, tables laden with food and followed by mass at St. Bridgett's Catholic church. We knew it could no longer really matter to the real person she was, yet we all felt keenly how bizarre a scene it was. That was our mother, still unable to join the consensual reality. That was Gram's beloved child who could not honor or reconcile with her, even in death.

After the church service, Gram's casket was driven to Abington and placed on the ground near the graves of her parents, Amanda and Tom and small brothers, Willie and Berty. A very kind minister that Gram had known briefly, spoke. Then we all sang her favorite hymns, "Lead Kindly Light" and "Abide With Me." Irene did not attend. Ironically, Gram's name was misspelled on her tombstone.

But, at last Annie was free of everyone else's needs and demands. At last she was free of the 'old organism,' as she called her body, with its confining blindness. The mystery was revealed and she could know everything.

I went home alone and cried. I begged her to forgive me for deserting her in her hour of need. And I heard her whisper, "Dot, dear, I understand." For the first time in months I felt a sense of peace again.

Georgie and her family returned to their summer home in Canada to recuperate. Shortly afterward, Georgie woke from a sound sleep. She felt impelled to go downstairs to the kitchen of the old farmhouse. When she got there, she saw Gram standing in the pantry. She had been able to keep her promise. She looked very much alive and well and now spoke clearly, in her dear, familiar voice.

"Georgianna," she said. "The end of life is life itself." Then she disappeared.

Georgie thought, "I must write this down." She got a piece of paper and wrote it down, went upstairs and fell back to sleep. The next morning, completely forgetting the incident, she was surprised to find the piece of paper with its statement, sitting in the pantry.

We have been trying to discern its meaning ever since. But even more important, we continue to be nourished by the teachings and example of this exceptional woman of unfailing love, Annie Benson Müller.

Last portrait of Annie at 92, taken by Georgianna.

ACKNOWLEDGMENTS

I wish to thank my children, family, and friends for encouraging me to document my grandmother's life. Also, thanks to Maine Media Women for pulling me out of the closet to call myself a writer out loud. I owe them many thanks for providing me with practical advice about the writing world—its walls, pits, and wastebaskets. Thank you to all the great writers whose books continue to inform and illuminate my work. And especially to all at Maine Authors Publishing & Cooperative for their efficient and courteous assistance with the myriad details required to see this dream beautifully realized.